SAM HOUSTON & NAPOLEON BONAPARTE MEET ON THE CIVIL WAR BATTLEFIELD

A TRUE STORY OF THE WALKER BROTHERS

BY

Edward Leo Semler Jr.

Copyright © 2017 by Edward Leo Semler Jr.

All rights reserved by the author.

First Edition: 2017

Library of Congress Control Number: 2017910912

ISBN: 978-0-692-91835-7

Printed in the United States of America

Cover picture is of Sam Houston Walker - more than likely at Fort Johnston in Shreveport, Louisiana.

To Sam Houston, Lewis, Napoleon Bonaparte, and descendants of the Walker family

Table of contents

Introduction	1
Before the war	9
1862	17
1863	41
1864	67
1865	87
After the war	91
In closing	103
References	107
About the author	109

Introduction

It seems like I've been exposed to the Civil War my entire life. I grew up in Northern Virginia, an area that was prominent during the war, surrounded by numerous battlefields. My father took our family on many occasions to some of the most famous battlefields in the area and probably the entire war, such as Gettysburg, Bull Run, and Antietam.

One memorable experience growing up was stopping for lunch at a pull-off on the Pennsylvania turnpike. We were somewhere a little north of the battlefields of Antietam and were making our usual trip to the Pittsburgh area to visit my grandparents. My mom always packed a picnic lunch, usually consisting of fried chicken and potato salad, and we would pull over and eat it along the way. My dad really didn't like the busy food and gas plazas and preferred the quiet roadside picnic pull-offs. He didn't have a particular spot to stop and would just pull over when we were hungry or he wanted a break from diving. So the pull-offs were different every time we stopped. And as my mom would prepare the meal, either on the tailgate of the station wagon or picnic table, if the pull-off had one, my brother, sisters, and I would wonder off into the nearby woods or fields and explore. On this memorable occasion, as we noodled around at the edge of a meadow, we came across 2 small headstones. Concealed in the summer growth, we didn't notice them until we were right on top of them. They had an arched top and were weathered stone, but the engraving was clear enough to read. Belonging to 2 Civil War soldiers, they were more than likely buried near where they had been killed in a skirmish. It struck me as odd at the time that they would be buried all by themselves in a place that probably only the landowner knew about. Now I know that was common in the war, and these 2 soldiers were lucky that their graves were even marked, as so many only had a wooden cross that rotted away in only a few years. As an adult I have made that trip up the turnpike countless times and have tried to find those 2 graves, with no luck. I guess they are lost to history, but not my memory.

I've toured Fort Sumter, and lived near Frederick, Maryland with the Monocacy and South Mountain battlefields in my backyard. I even wrote a book, *"The Three Gunsallus Brothers – Fighting for Pennsylvania During the Civil War."* That book was about my great-great grandfather and two of his brothers. It was a fun book to research and had a compelling story about how they fought their way through the war.

This book has just as compelling a story. I think it really demonstrates how the American Civil War not only divided the country, but also families. The Walker Brothers; Samuel, Lewis, and Napoleon, were normal men of their time, trying to make a living for themselves and caring for their families. But as battles over politics, sovereignty, and slavery divided the nation they had to choose a side. The war engulfed the country and affected everyone.

You may be asking yourself why I chose the Walker Brothers. Well just as John Gunsallus in *"The Three Gunsallus Brothers"* is my great-great grandfather, Samuel Houston Walker is my wife Jana's great-great grandfather. And in the Walker family Samuel's (Sam) life story as a Texan, preacher, and soldier are legendary. With a name like Sam Houston and eventually living in Texas, he had a lot to live up to! I had known for a while that Sam Houston had fought during the Civil War and had done a little research for the family a few years before writing this book. I decided to revisit his military career and while noodling around doing some genealogy research on him I came across the fact that one of his brothers, Napoleon Bonaparte, also fought during the Civil War. This really intrigued me and got me interested in what his other four brothers were up to during this time period. And low and behold I found that his brother Lewis also fought, along with several current and future brothers-in-law. And to make things even more interesting, Sam Houston and Napoleon Bonaparte actually fought on the same battlefield. So I knew I had to research this further, which led me to writing this book.

As with *"The Three Gunsallus Brothers,"* this book could not have been compiled without the enormous amount of time and effort spent by those I give credit to in the reference section of this book. People and organizations that have taken the time to research and document Confederate and Union battle and regiment information, genealogy and military records, and so much other information that has helped me to tell the story of the Walker Brothers.

It's not easy to go back over 150 years and piece together detailed events. Of course, everyone who was living at the time, plus their children, and their children's children – have long passed away. So no one is around who either remembers or can answer questions about what Sam Houston or his brothers did during the Civil War. And how reliable is the verbal information passed down from family member to family member? I found that when I was researching *"The Three Gunsallus Brothers"* that there was a lot of family folk lore that was just plain wrong. My favorite, which we all believed, was that we had 5 relatives that fought at the Battle of Gettysburg. And that only one survived, because he was sent home on leave to be at his dying mother's bedside. The truth, that I uncovered while doing my research, was that we only had one relative that fought at Gettysburg and he survived the battle. And the relative that had the sick mother and was requesting leave to be at her bedside happened later in the war at the Battle of Petersburg, and his mother survived and died many years after the war. So you have to verify everything that gets passed down verbally over several generations in the family!

The Walker Brothers did not leave many documents to help me personalize or detail their time in the service, such as diaries or letters home - that I am aware of. So how do I know what I'm about to tell you is true, or is at least based on facts?

I was able to obtain copies of Napoleon's, Lewis's, and Samuel's, military records from the National Archives. Those records, along with other documentation had a majority of their Company Muster Roll Cards. These cards identify on a monthly basis which company and regiment they were attached to, if they were present or absent for any period, special details they were assigned, promotions, pay, and so on. So by following the company and regiment they were attached to, I can subsequently follow them. As an example; I have a Company Muster Roll Card showing Lewis was attached to Company A of the 48th Regiment Mounted Infantry, Kentucky Volunteers. It states that he was in fact present with his unit on March and April of 1863. But, he was on leave from the 31st of March to the 15th of April. So I can place him with any action that took place with his company during March and April with the exception of the time he is noted as being on leave. Samuel's is a little bit harder because his regiment didn't keep good records, and what was kept may have been destroyed during or after the war. But I was lucky enough to come across an autobiography summary given by Samuel stating, among other things, that he fought in the battles that I have placed him at in this book. And he gives a brief description of his war service. So with this type of information I can safely say he was where I have placed him.

| W. | 48 | Ky. |

Lewis Walker

Prvt., Co. A, 48 Reg't Kentucky Infantry.

Appears on

Company Muster Roll

for _Mar. & April_, 1864

Present or absent _Present_

Stoppage, $ ___ 100 for ___

Due Gov't, $ ___ 100 for ___

Remarks: _At home on furlough since the 31st day of March 1864, to the 15th day of April 1864, since which time he has been with his Company._

Book mark: ___

H. L. Thomas
Copyist

(858)

Lewis Walker's Company Muster Roll Card

But even with all this information there are still gray areas that have been lost to time. When I encountered these situations I used the facts I had to logically determine what probably transpired. So this story is based on fact, with an occasional educated guess. An example would be the fact that I have no record of Samuel leaving his regiment while fighting in 1864. But his second child was born in October of 1864. If that child was his – and there is no evidence to the contrary, he would have had to spend time with his wife around January of that year. And since it is not likely she would have left home to track him down in a war zone, he must have gone to her.

I was also able to locate photographs from the Library of Congress and other sources that depict some of the major milestones in this story. Photography was in its infancy during the 1860's so they are not the clearest, but they certainly provide a visual record of what the brothers actually saw.

Finally, books and articles that I read, researching this book and as a hobby, seemed to get into the weeds about what every regiment, division, corps, and general was doing at the same time as their subject. I realize that their intention was to give the reader a broad understanding of what was going on surrounding their subject, but I found this very confusing and distracting. Especially when you are following three men, two on different sides, and each in a different regiment. So I tried to limit this broader view of the war and its leaders, and instead kept the focus of the story on the Walker Brothers and their companies and regiments.

For instance, at the Battle of Helena, Arkansas Lieutenant General Theophilus H. Holmes moved his Army of Arkansas which consisted of several Divisions, to include Sam Houston's, against Major General Benjamin Prentiss and his Army of Eastern Arkansas. Each of these armies consisted of 3 to 4 divisions, 6 or more battalions, around 30 regiments and 100's of companies. I just focus on what Sam Houston and his company and regiment were doing. And maybe the company and regiment he was immediately engaged with in fighting.

I hope you appreciate the simplification of army, division, battalion, and regimental movements. And by all means if you're interested in the full scale of each army's movements, it only takes a few minutes to search the internet for the full story.

Before the war

The Walker Brothers were the sons of James and Charlotte, who were simple Tennessee farmers. James was a veteran of the War of 1812 and served in the Virginia Militia. After the war he relocated to Tennessee where he and Charlotte married in 1824. The two of them started a family and moved around Tennessee for several years. By 1850 they had settled in Macon County, Tennessee, which is north of Nashville and a stone's throw from the Kentucky state line. According to the 1850 census all 10 of their children were still living at home, along with their oldest son's wife. Life for the Walkers would have been consumed with farming their land. And the more hands able to help the better because all the farming had to be done by hand or using horse drawn equipment. And if that wasn't hard enough, having 13 people living in a single farm house must have had that house nearly busting at the seams. Not to mention no electricity, no indoor plumbing, and water was drawn from a hand pump outside. All day long a cooking fire had to be kept going, and in the winter months fire wood had to be collected and the fireplace stoked producing heat to survive. So I imagine that when an opportunity to move on presented itself, it was acted upon. Although emotionally difficult and less hands for the same work, it would have meant a little more space and probably a little more to eat at meal times for those left behind.

By 1861 most of the older children had left home and ventured out to make their own mark on the expanding nation. This left the homestead in the hands of James, Charlotte, and several of the younger children.

Although the entire Walker family certainly experienced hardships and had compelling stories during the Civil War, this book focuses on the experiences of Sam, Lewis, and Napoleon.

Sam Houston Walker was no doubt given his name for the famous Texan, Sam Houston. The famous Houston, like Sam's father, was a Virginian, spent time in Tennessee, and fought in the War of 1812. Sam Houston Walker was born on the 22nd of December 1829 and was the youngest of the three brothers to fight in the war. He was able to read and write and had some schooling. His biography tells us he traveled a bit in his younger years in the surrounding counties and across the border into Kentucky, but stayed relatively close to home. That is until he and Napoleon, in their early 20s, decided to strike out on their own. They moved nearly 600 miles away to work on farms near Sarcoxie, Missouri. Sam wound up living and working as a farm hand on the farm of John King. Soon after, he met and married Cilia Fishburn in 1855. A deeply religious man he joined the White Oak Baptist Church there in town. In 1858 he and Cilia packed up their belongings and moved further south to Elm Springs, Arkansas. Near extended family they set up house and had their first child, Alexander, in 1860.

Lewis Walker didn't have an obvious historical namesake like his two brothers had. Born on the 25th of January 1829 he was less than a year older then Sam. As an adult he was 5 foot 10 inches tall, dark complected, with blue eyes. He was able to read and write, so more than likely he had attended school. He probably stayed at home until he married Mary Goober in 1858 and settled down in Millersburg, Tennessee a little south of the family homestead in Macon County. Around 1861 Lewis moved his wife and first child north across the state border into Kentucky and continued his trade as a farmer.

Napoleon Bonaparte Walker was obviously named after the famous French military leader. The Frenchman's popularity in America was high during the War of 1812 because he was also at odds with the mutually hated British. Napoleon Bonaparte Walker, the oldest of the three brothers, was born the 13th of May 1827 in Knox County, Tennessee. Napoleon grew up to be 5 foot 6 inches tall, which was an average height for the time. He had auburn hair, blue eyes and was of a light complexion. He more than likely attended school because, like his younger brothers, he could also read and write.

In the early 1850's, and in his 20's, he left home and headed to Missouri with his brother Sam. He found work as a farm hand, living and working on the farm of J.B. Howard in McDonald County, Missouri, which was about 25 miles from where Sam Houston was living and working.

I'm not really sure what it was that lured Napoleon and Sam Houston almost 600 miles to the west and the farms of

Missouri. More than likely they joined people flocking to the west during the 1850's in search of a better living and perhaps some adventure. At the time Western Missouri was the last stop before entering the Unorganized Territories and Indian Territory. So there were lots of opportunities in this expanding part of the country. After looking at the 1850 & 60 censuses I found that there were several Walkers who were neighbors to the farms where Napoleon and Sam Houston were living and working. Perhaps they were related. So they may have been drawn out by tales from their extended family about the opportunities in Missouri. They also may have given them an initial foothold until they found work and boarding at the neighboring farms.

In 1861, as I mentioned previously, the country was taking sides on the issues of politics, slavery and a state's individual right to govern itself. Arguably there were many other underlying issues that drove such a wedge between men, states, and the federal government. Although slavery was a predominant reason for states wanting to secede from the United States, there were also Union states that had legalized slavery. So slavery wasn't the defining issue for siding with the Confederate States or United States.

Along with Tennessee the states that would form the Confederate States of America and secede from the United States were Texas, Louisiana, Mississippi, Alabama, Georgia, South Carolina, Florida, Arkansas, North Carolina, Virginia, and the Indian and Arizona Territories. Although these were Confederate States they also had pockets of Union supporters and therefore provided soldiers that fought on the side of the United States.

Missouri, Kentucky, West Virginia, Maryland, and Delaware were considered boarder states and neutral. Even still, they all had men fighting on both sides of the war.

To sort of get a mindset on what might be driving the brothers thought process on these issues I looked at what the state they were born and raised in leaned towards during this time period. Tennessee was a slave state leading up to the Civil War, meaning slavery was legal. Although heavily depending on slave labor to support its economy Tennessee became somewhat split when it came time to take up sides as the talk of war neared. Most of the state naturally supported the secession and nearly 136,000 Tennessee men fought for the Confederacy. But the eastern tip of the state did end up supporting the north and approximately 31,000 white and 6,700 black men fought for the Union. This was more men than all the other Confederate states combined provided to the Union.

Even though the Walker Brothers were raised in Tennessee and surrounded by slave labor for most of their lives leading up to the war, they themselves didn't own any slaves. Possibly because they were poor subsistence farmers themselves.

Then when the Confederates attacked Fort Sumter, South Carolina in April of 1861 the country was thrown into war. So what side do you think the brothers took up arms with?

Samuel Houston Walker

Lewis Walker

Napoleon Bonaparte Walker

1862

Napoleon was the first to pick a side. Working in south western Missouri as a farm hand he found himself in the Confederate stronghold of the state. Opposed to the Confederacy he crossed over into neighboring Kansas and headed north towards Leavenworth. Just south of the Leavenworth city limits he enlisted with the Union Army at Camp Deitzler on the 17th of March 1862. He signed up for 3 years with Company K of the 6th Kansas Cavalry as a private. As was the going rate he received a $100 sign up bonus, referred to as a "bounty." This was a lot of money and was supposed to be spread out in payments over his enlistment. The monthly pay for a private was $13 a month so the bounty alone equaled almost a year's wages.

The 6th Kansas Cavalry, a long standing Army unit, was reforming further south of Camp Deitzler at Fort Scott, Kansas. Located on the Kansas & Missouri border Fort Scott was only about 100 miles from where Napoleon had lived in Missouri. The Cavalry Regiment was in the midst of discharging several companies of veterans whose enlistments had expired. As they reorganized they hired on new recruits like Napoleon.

Napoleon Bonaparte Walker's Muster Card

At the age of 34 Napoleon was by no means considered a young man and was embarking on a tough lifestyle as a cavalryman. The 6th Kansas Cavalry spent most of their time scouting, sleeping under the stars and braving the elements.

There was however, no time to contemplate as Company K moved out 2 days later on the 19th of March to Carthage, Missouri - a distance of 65 miles. Having to bed down on the cold, 30 degree March ground Napoleon was probably wondering what he had gotten himself into.

On the 26th the company moved 16 miles away to Bowers Mills performing scouting duties in the area until the 3rd of April. Then they moved back to Fort Scott, which would provide a roof over their heads and a straw mattress to lay down on. On the 21st they were ordered to Coldwater Grove, Kansas to rejoin the regiment and arrived the 2nd of May. They mounted up and moved 16 miles to Paola, Kansas which was the regiment's headquarters on the 4th of May. Enjoying warmer and milder weather the living conditions were getting easier but not any less dangerous. While on scout duty Company K lost Private John Mulvaney when his horse was spooked and darted away, dragging him to death.

On the 27th Company K left the regiment and marched the 65 miles back to Fort Scott. Breaking up into individual companies was common for the 6th Kansas. The regiment was made up of 10 companies and each company had generally around 100 men when at full strength. So individual companies, or groups of companies were routinely detailed to special duties or assignments. After restocking supplies the company was assigned to scouting west into Indian Territory (present day state of Oklahoma), where it remained until it returned to Fort Scott on the 14th of June.

Although Napoleon and Company K had not encountered any Confederates during their scouting to date, there was plenty going on in the area. Local Confederate militias and guerrilla forces were active and had engaged other companies belonging to the 6th Kansas Cavalry and other Union forces in Missouri and along the Kansas border. Beside the Battle at Pea Ridge in March of 1862 there had been no major battles fought in the vicinity to date, but there had been numerous skirmishes. And the Confederate Guerrillas operating in the area were getting to be notoriously ruthless. As evidenced by what happened to one of Napoleon's fellow Company K comrades, Private Abraham Woodall. After deserting Company K on the 30th of June from Fort Scott, he was killed by guerrillas for having sided with the Union.

Fort Scott, Kansas[13]

Fort Scott had by far the best facilities Napoleon would encounter during most of the war. The fort covered a wide area and had officers' quarters, barracks, hospital, mess house, commissary, stables, and adjacent town. Getting back to Fort Scott after scouting out in basically the wilderness of Indian Territory must have been something to look forward to.

Cavalrymen fighting for the Union were usually provided horses, but if you had your own the army would reimburse you for it. The Confederates on the other hand didn't provide or reimburse their men for providing a horse. In July Napoleon purchased his own horse and saddlery and was reimbursed for doing so. The most common reason for providing your own horse came down to personal preference. Government horses were okay but not the best, and you took what you were given.

Men spending all day with a horse usually wanted a quality animal they could trust, and provided their own if they could.

As the July summer sun was heating up, so was the war. And Napoleon's brother Sam Houston picked his side. Unlike his brother Napoleon, Sam chose the Confederacy! Traveling from his home in Elm Springs, Arkansas to Camp Cedar near Little Rock, Arkansas he joined Company A of the 2nd Regiment Missouri Infantry on the 21st of July. This regiment would later be known as the 11th Regiment Missouri Infantry. And again unlike his brother, Sam signed up for the duration of the war. I'm sure at the time he had no idea it would drag on for nearly 3 more years. Not making as much as his brother, Sam's monthly pay as a private was $11 a month. And like his Union brother he was supposed to get paid every two months. But both would soon find out that it could stretch into 3 or 4 months before the pay officer caught up to them with their money.

Joining a Confederate Missouri Regiment in Arkansas sounds a little odd, but was common at the time. This was because of all the turmoil going on in neighboring Missouri. Union forces had pushed Missouri Confederate sympathizers south into Arkansas. Confederate forces from Missouri were constantly crossing back and forth from Missouri and Arkansas to avoid the Union Army and recruited as they moved.

(Confederate.)

W | 1 1 | Mo.

S. H. Walker

Pvt., Co. A, 2 Reg't Missouri Infantry.

Appears on

Company Muster Roll

of the organization named above,

for July 21 to Oct 31, 186 2.

Enlisted:
When July 21, 186 .
Where Camp Cedar
By whom Col Burns
Period 3 yrs.

Last paid:
By whom
To what time , 186 .

Present or absent Present

Remarks:

Hunter's Battalion Missouri Infantry, consisting of seven companies which had previously served as cavalry, was organized August 31, 1862. The battalion was increased by the addition of other companies and organized as the 2d (also known as Hunter's) Regiment Missouri Infantry September 15, 1862; its designation was changed to the 8th Regiment Missouri Infantry and finally to the 11th Regiment Missouri Infantry.

Book mark:

J. M. Pinsel

(642) Copyist.

Sam Houston Walker's Company Muster Card

Immediately after joining, Sam Houston and the 25 men that had thus far been recruited to Company A, left Little Rock and headed to Van Buren, Arkansas. Located in the northwest corner of the state Van Buren bordered Confederate friendly Indian Territory. At this point in the war Company A was operating as a cavalry company and able to make good speed. On the 28th of July they headed north into Missouri hugging the Kansas border. Their mission was to head north 250 miles to Lone Jack, Missouri and rendezvous with Colonel Coffee's regiment and other Confederate Militias operating in the area.

After replenishing supplies once again at Fort Scott, Napoleon and Company K headed 170 miles south to Fort Gibson in Indian Territory. Fort Gibson was a very important outpost on the Arkansas and Neosho Rivers. Running east, the Arkansas ran to Fort Smith, which was currently in Confederate hands, and to Little Rock, Arkansas, which was the Union capital of the state. Running north, the Neosho River ran all the way into Kansas. These river ways would become crucial to keeping the Union Army supplied.

Fort Gibson was also in a chain of older pre-war forts, like Fort Scott, and Fort Leavenworth, which were established to enforce the Indian boundaries to the west and enforce trade and preserve peace on the western frontier. So when the Civil War broke out these Union forts became strategically important because they bordered the Confederacy's north and western border. Although these forts were a safe haven, in military terms, for the Union men, they were certainly not safe from disease. Unfortunately more men from the 6th Kansas Cavalry died at these forts from disease then actually died in combat. Illnesses such as chronic diarrhea, pneumonia, fever, measles, and the mumps would claim 3 officers and 140 enlisted men during the war. Compared to the 4 officers and 81 enlisted men who would be killed in action or eventually die from their wounds. And this wasn't an anomaly with the 6th Kansas, just about every Civil War company on both sides lost more men to disease and illness then to combat fatalities.

Company K remained in the vicinity of Fort Gibson scouting until the 1st of August when they broke camp and headed back to Fort Scott, arriving on the 8th of August.

On the 10th of August the entire 6th Cavalry mounted up and headed north in pursuit of Colonel Coffee and the Confederate Militias in Missouri as another smaller Union force was dispatched from Lexington, Missouri. Now, two brothers on opposite sides of the war were unknowingly heading towards each other.

Sam Houston and Company A met up with the militia of Colonel Coffee on the outskirts of Lone Jack, Missouri before either detachment of the Union Army arrived. Meanwhile another group of Confederates and guerrillas were also forming near Lone Jack. The smaller Union force coming from Lexington arrived on the 15th of August and established themselves in the town itself. Not waiting for Napoleon and his Union reinforcements, the Union men from Lexington attacked the second set of Confederates. Outnumbering the Union by 2 to 1 the Confederates drove the Union men from Lexington into a retreat after 5 hours of brutal fighting in the town center. Arriving late in the battle Sam Houston and his Confederate contingent saw little action. The 6th Kansas Cavalry arrived the following day. Now evenly matched Sam Houston and the Confederates decided they were too far north and didn't like the matchup. So Napoleon commenced to follow his brother Sam and the rest of the withdrawing Confederates south. The lead Union scouts caught up with lagging Confederates and skirmished at Coon Creek, Missouri on the 24th of August with two men from Company C and one from Company F of the 6th Kansas being killed in action. After the skirmish the chase continued as they pursued the Confederates 120 miles south as far as Carthage, Missouri when the 6th Kansas were ordered back to Fort Scott. Arriving back to the fort on the 26th of August Napoleon and the 6th Kansas regrouped and resupplied.

A personal account of the aftermath of the battle was given by Stephen B. Elkins, who would go on to become the Secretary of War;

"I saw one battle while in the service, that of Lone Jack, and a most awful battle it was. Col. Emory S. Foster had a Union regiment which was attacked by the brother of Senator Cockrell, but Foster thought the Confederates were the guerrilla hands who raised the black flag, and never gave any quarter. So he refused to surrender, and every one of his officers was picked off. The guerrillas were victorious. I went over the battlefield afterward, the blood, the cries for water and death, the naked bodies stripped of their clothing, the dead horses which served for ramparts, gave me a disgust for war,

which makes it seem strange that I am here at the head of the war department of this great government."[23]

The Battle of Lone Jack was costly for both sides. It's hard to get an accurate casualty count because each side's after action report differs greatly. It's generally understood that the Union lost about 175 killed or wounded and the Confederates about 125. Both brothers missed the major fighting, but there's no way to know if they were in close combat during the retreat and chase at Coon Creek. But after seeing the aftermath of their first battle I'm sure neither would be looking forward to the next major fight.

Just an interesting note for John Wayne fans or movie trivia buffs. In the movie "True Grit," Rooster Cogburn, states in conversation that he lost his eye fighting for the Confederacy at the Battle of Lone Jack. Hence he wore a black eye patch.[19]

Sam Houston and the Confederate force continued heading further south back into Arkansas and held up in Bentonville on the 22nd of August. Although they retreated, the fighting at Lone Jack was considered a Confederate victory by historians because of their first day victory, Sam Houston's retreating company sustained a lieutenant killed and 3 privates wounded.

Heading south on the 1st of September the 6th Kansas Cavalry as part of the 1st Kansas Brigade headed into Confederate held territory to scout for the enemy. Even seemingly simple and everyday chores can be deadly while scouting. One tragic example was that of Private Michael Twoomey of Company G who drowned on September 18th while watering his horse.

As Napoleon scouted, a Confederate force had secured the nearby town of Newtonia, Missouri and its vital grain mill. Napoleon and the Union force were redirected to engage the enemy in Newtonia and secure that mill. Heading towards Newtonia on the 19th they were attacked by harassing Confederate Guerrillas and a private from Company B was killed. These bands of guerrillas operated with "strike and flee" tactics. They would ambush or strike a Union outfit and then flee before the Union men could regroup and give chase. And it was hard to even give chase because the guerrillas would blend right in with the local population. So it was hard to tell who was friend or foe.

At 7am on the morning of September 30th the two armies engaged at Newtonia, Missouri. This is one of the few Civil War battles in which Native American Indians played a major role. The Union force had two regiments of mixed Indians and the Confederates a regiment each of Choctaw and Chickasaw Indians.

The battle waged back and forth as the fighting centered on the Prichie Farmhouse and their barn. But Confederate Indian reinforcements caused the Union force along with the 6th Kansas Cavalry to retreat in disorganized haste. They were driven north about 10 miles to Sarcoxie, Sam Houston's old stomping grounds in Missouri. Several days later Union reinforcements arrived and the tide was turned - the Union was able to retake Newtonia and hold it. During the fighting Company C lost 2 men to enemy fire. Most of the Confederate force fled south into northern Arkansas. Although initially a

Confederate victory, they were unable to maintain control of the area because of the increasing number of Union troops converging on the town, so they moved south and gave up the town and mill.

After the Battles at Lone Jack and Newtonia the Confederates were demonstrating an awkward trend of winning the battle but not being able to maintain control over what they had fought so hard for. Superior Union manning and armament, along with better supply lines were making it difficult on the Confederates. But the Confederates were trying to even the score by harassing the Union supply lines.

Confederate held Prichie Barn[20]

After securing Newtonia the 6th Kansas headed south on the 4th of October looking for the enemy. Minor encounters on the 22nd and 23rd of October near Mayville, Arkansas left two scouts from Company A dead. As they scouted for the enemy Napoleon was promoted from private to wagoner.

The role of a wagoner was to transport the supplies needed by Company K. Napoleon was now responsible for driving the wagon, maintaining it, feeding and caring for the mule team that pulled it, ensuring that it was loaded properly, and ensuring that its cargo reached its destination safely. The cargo could be anything that Company K required; food, medicines, weapons, ammunition, clothing, shelter tents, tools, the soldiers' knack sacks, officers' luggage, company records, and anything else the company needed. Usually when the company would engage the enemy the cavalrymen would leave most of their personal belongings with the wagoner who stayed back in the rear. This would allow the cavalrymen to move faster and lighter.

As Napoleon and the Union force moved south in search of the enemy they constantly had forward scouts probing the country side for the Confederate's main force. Private Levi Howard of Company K was killed near Cato, Kansas in a skirmish on the 8th of November. Then on the 20th the 6th Kansas Cavalry performing lead scout duty encountered Confederate pickets north of Fort Smith, Arkansas. Fort Smith was one of many forts taken over by the Confederates at the start of the war, mainly because they were in Confederate held territory. The larger Confederate forces on the other hand, were on their way north in anticipation of driving the Union Army out of Arkansas and back into Missouri.

Heading towards each other were Napoleon's Union force of 5,000 and an 11,000 man Confederate Army. But on the 28th of November the Union force surprised an outnumbered 2,000 man Confederate Calvary advance scouting force at Cane Hill, Arkansas. The Confederates immediately moved to the high ground and took a stand. As Union forces pushed up towards the Confederates it was noticed that they had held back a rear guard. Seeing this as a threat to the Union advance, three companies of the 6th Kansas, which were likewise being held in reserve, volunteered to swing around and attack the Confederate rear guard. One of these companies was Napoleon's.

The Commanding Officer of the Union force, General James G. Blunt, described the scene in a letter to his superior;

"I called for volunteers to make a charge. Three companies of the Sixth Kansas, nearest at hand, responded promptly to the call, and, under command of their three field officers, Colonel Judson, Lieutenant-Colonel Jewell, and Major Campbell, dashed on the rear of the rebel column, cutting and shooting them down with sabers, carbines, and revolvers. The charge continued for about half a mile down the valley, to a point where it converged in a funnel shape, terminating in a narrow defile. At this point a large body of the enemy were in ambush in front and upon the flanks, where cavalry could not approach, with their battery also masked in front. As soon as the party we were pursuing had passed through the defile, they opened upon us a most destructive fire, which, for the moment, caused my men to recoil and give back, in spite of my own

efforts and those of other officers to rally them; whereas, if they had, after receiving the enemy's fire, passed on 200 or 300 yards, we would have secured, in a moment more, what we so much coveted – the enemy's artillery. Emboldened by their success in defending the defile and checking our advance, they raised a wild yell and advanced toward us. With the aid of Colonel Judson, Major Campbell, and Captains Greeno and Mefford, I succeeded in rallying the three companies of the Sixth Kansas, who had suffered severely in the charge, and formed them across the valley, and the four howitzers, coming up at the same time and opening on the enemy with shell, soon forced them to retire.

Yet they seemed determined to dispute the passage of the defile to which I have referred – a position admirably adapted for defense; and beyond which, as I afterward learned, there was a wide and open valley; hence their obstinate resistance at this point, in order to save their guns. I resolved, however, at all hazards to force my way through this gorge, and, as darkness was approaching and I had no time to get up infantry and send them out upon the flanks, I prepared to make an assault in front. Loading the four howitzers and one section of Rabb's battery with double canister, I ordered them up by hand, in battery, with the three companies of the Sixth Kansas with Sharps' carbines advancing in line in rear. I had directed that not a gun should be fired until I gave the word"[21]

As Napoleon's comrades prepared for their counter attack, and the sun was about to set on the battlefield, the Confederates came forward with a flag of truce. Stunned, the Union officer in charge thought it might be a trick. But all the Confederates wanted was to withdraw with their arms and wounded. Since darkness was upon them the truce was agreed upon and both sides collected their wounded.

The engagement lasted for 9 hours until sundown when the Union pushed the Confederate Cavalrymen back towards Fort Smith. Realizing they were overextending their supply line and ability to receive reinforcements the Union detachment held their position. The Confederate Cavalrymen regrouped at Fort Smith with their main force of 11,000 men. The entire engagement cost the Union 4 men killed with 36 wounded and the Confederates sustained 45 casualties. Of those Union losses the 6th Kansas lost 3 men from Company A. And from Napoleon's Company K 1st Sergeant George Ritchie was mortally wounded, 2nd Lieutenant John Harris was severely wounded in the neck, and Sergeant Silas Maupin was wounded.

While Napoleon was fighting in northern Arkansas Sam Houston was a little further south and in the midst of transferring units. As the Battle of Cane Hill raged on, Sam Houston volunteered for the 9th Battalion Missouri Sharpshooters on the 28th of November. This battalion was also referred to as "Pindall's Sharpshooters" in recognition of the Battalion Commander, Major Lebbeus A. Pindall. Sam was assigned to Company B which was predominantly made up of volunteers from his previous regiment, so he transferred with a lot of his friends. In fact it's interesting to note that one of the privates that he served previously with was made a Captain and commanded Sam's new Company B. Now, if you know about the military rank structure this is an unusually huge jump in ranks. Being a military man myself I can only surmise he had the highest respect from his men in Company B for having been a low level enlisted man who had walked in their shoes.

9th Battalion Missouri Sharpshooters battle flag, which was never lost in battle[4]

Waiting for reinforcements and supplies the Union Army, along with the 6th Kansas held at Cane Hill and kept an eye on the large Confederate force massing near Fort Smith.

After transferring to Pindall's Sharpshooters Sam and his new battalion also moved up to join the growing Confederate Army near Fort Smith. At the same time Napoleon and Company K were detailed to a solemn duty. During the fighting at Cane Hill the 6th Kansas Cavalry lost their second in command, Lieutenant Colonel Lewis Jewell. Mortally wounded in the hip during the ambushed attack on the Confederate rear guard on the 28th he succumbed to his wounds on the 30th. The loss of Lieutenant Colonel Jewell must have been especially emotional for Napoleon because he had personally enlisted Napoleon into Company K. Napoleon and Company K left the rest of the 6th Kansas on the 3rd of December to escort his body back to Fort Scott, Kansas.

As Napoleon and Company K escorted the body of Lieutenant Colonel Jewell, Sam Houston and the Confederate Army were heading north again, en masse to finally push the Union Army out of Arkansas. As one of the first major battles in the area was about to take place, the Walker Brothers were heading in opposite directions. And by divine intervention their battalions would meet head to head without the brothers having to face each other.

The 11,000 men of the Confederacy reached Prairie Grove, Arkansas first, which was just 10 miles from the previous fighting at Cane Hill. The now nearly 9,000 man Union Army shifted from its position at Cane Hill to engage the enemy. This was winter and the temperatures were dropping into the 30's at night and only getting into the high 40's during the day.

That's rough weather to be sleeping out under the stars and to have to fight in.

To prepare his men for the upcoming battle the Commanding Officer of the Confederate Army, Major General T. C Hindman sent this proclamation out to be read to his men on the 4th of December;

"Soldiers: From the commencement to the end of the battle, bear constantly in mind what I now urge upon you:

First. Never fire because your comrades do; nor because the enemy does; nor because you happen to see the enemy; nor for the sake of firing rapidly. Always wait till you are certainly within the range of your gun, then single out your man, take deliberate aim, as low down as the knee, and fire.

Second. When occasion offers, be certain to pick off the enemy's officers, especially the mounted ones, and kill his artillery horses.

Third. Do not shout, except when you charge the enemy. As a general thing, keep silent, that orders may be heard. Obey the orders of your officers, but pay no attention to idle rumors or the words of unauthorized persons.

Fourth. Do not stop with your wounded comrades; the surgeons and infirmary corps will take care of them; do you go forward and avenge them.

Fifth. Do not break ranks to plunder. If we whip the enemy, all he has will be ours; if not, the spoil will be of no benefit to us.

Plunderers and stragglers will be put to death upon the spot. File-closers are especially charged with this duty. The cavalry in rear will likewise attend to it.

Remember that the enemy you engage has no feeling of mercy of kindness toward you. His ranks are made up of Pin Indians, free negroes, Southern tories, Kentucky jayhawkers, and hired Dutch cut-throats. These broody ruffians have invaded your country; stolen and destroyed your property; murdered your neighbors; outraged your woman; driven your children from their homes, and defiled the graves of your kindred. If each man of you will do what I have urged upon you, we will utterly destroy them. We can do this; our country will be ruined if we fail. A just God will strengthen our arms and give us a glorious victory." [21]

As I read that I thought that it could have just as likely been written for pirates! But you have to place it in the context of who he was delivering it to. A lot of the men under his command, and fighting for the Confederacy, were non-regular army militias and guerrillas. Men such as Frank & Jesse James, and the Younger Brothers. Men who would go on to form the Jesse James Gang and rob and kill at will after the war. During the war they fought under William Quantrill and his guerrilla militia. They were at Lone Jack and were also here for this battle.

These men also had no military training and went straight from plowing a field to fighting in a war. Unlike the Union Army where men were somewhat trained and everyone fell into some sort of enlistment contract or were drafted, these Confederate non-regulars fought at will and the way they wanted to. So here at the last minute he is having to tell them how to fight and behave.

On the 7th the two armies engaged. Meeting on the Confederate's left flank Sam Houston's Sharpshooters were pitted directly at Napoleon's remaining 6th Kansas Cavalry. As they battled each other in brutal and deadly combat all day the entire battlefield lay in a stalemate. The last push of the day, and the battle, was from Sam Houston's Confederates on the left flank as they charged across open ground. Once again Union General Blunt in a letter to his superior described the attack that Sam Houston endured;

"Learning that a heavy force was massing on my right with a view of turning my flank, I immediately withdrew Tenney's battery, and proceeded with it to an open field on the right, at the same time directing the infantry to withdraw from the wood, in order to draw the enemy from under cover and within range of my artillery. On reaching the open field on their right, just alluded to, I discovered the entire division of General Frost [The division Sam Houston was with] advanced to the edge of the timber, and 200 yards distant. They opened upon us a fierce fire from Enfield rifles, and were in the act of throwing down the fence to make an assault on the battery, which had no support except my own staff and body guard; but Lieutenant Tenney, with commendable promptness, wheeled his guns into position, when their destructive fire of canister and shell soon sent the rebel hordes back under cover of the wood."[21]

Just as Sam Houston was driven back the sun was setting. Exhausted, out of food, and nearly out of ammunition, the Confederate Army drifted back from the fighting and gave the Union a victory.

The initial casualty reports were enormous and claimed well over 1,000 Confederate dead as they were left to the Union Army to bury. But the official after action totals placed the Union losses at 175 men killed in action, 813 wounded, and 263 missing. The Confederates had 164 killed in action, 817 wounded, and 336 missing. A large number of the wounded would later die. Sam Houston's Company B had the man that carried their regimental colors, Sergeant Alfred Hamilton, wounded and one man from Company A taken prisoner. If there was ever any doubt that Sam Houston was in the thick of the fighting, that doubt has now been erased. Though Sam reported he left the battlefield unhurt, he was undoubtedly shaken. The Sharpshooters now marched south to Fort Smith where his company's Lieutenant, Gus Parsons, passed away from an illness. Then in late December they marched on to Lewisburg.

Napoleon reached Fort Scott on the 11th of December happy to be in a warm place, out of the elements, and off the frozen ground. But the luxury of having a warm roof over his head was short lived. After loading up with supplies Company K headed back to escorting a supply wagon train and to catch up with the rest of the 6th Kansas Cavalry. As was to be expected, the winter conditions slowed the wagon train's progress. Along with deaths from pneumonia there was always the threat of ambush from Confederate guerrillas operating in the area. And guerrillas hit the wagon train in Neosho, Missouri on the 27th of December killing Sergeant Zaccheus Hudson. Finally on the 31st Company K delivered the supply train to the 6th Kansas at Rhea Mills, Arkansas.

1863

Sam Houston's wife and son lived in Elm Springs, Arkansas which was just 22 miles north of the deadly fighting at Prairie Grove. With the war in his front yard and his homestead in Union hands, Sam felt that his family needed to relocate and get out of the war zone. So he directed them to move to Red River, Texas. This Confederate stronghold was west of the fighting and bordered Confederate friendly Indian Territory. I don't have a definitive answer as to why he chose Texas. My research indicates that he did not have family there to send her to. However, there were several men in his company from Red River, Texas. I can only speculate that he sent his family to stay with the family of one of his friends. His only other option would have been to send them to either his parents or her parents. It was just as dangerous at his parents' home in Macon, Tennessee. Although a Confederate county it was in the war zone and bordered a strong Union Army operating north in Kentucky. His wife's parents were from Missouri, just east of Joplin. But just like Elm Springs, it was right in the middle of active fighting and had a strong Union Army operating there.

Napoleon on the other hand was single and had nothing to worry about except his next meal and a warm place to sleep.

He and Company K were assigned on the 8th of January to Colonel Phillips and his Indian Brigade. This detail was twofold; first to provide much needed food, supplies, and protection to the Native American Indians and white settlers siding with the Union in Indian Territory. And second, to organize Indian regiments to fight for the Union. As I mentioned earlier this is present day Oklahoma and at the time was pretty much a Confederate friendly area. All the major Indian tribes in this area had signed treaties, supported, and were fighting for the Confederate cause. You may be asking yourself why the Indians were supporting the Confederacy. Well it's not a widely known fact, but some of the major tribes owned slaves and supported slavery. Others thought they would get a better deal with land and sovereignty from the Confederate States then with the United States, who had already proven treacherous and banished them to the west.

It was a tough time to be out in the elements, sleeping on the ground with just a tent over you – if you were lucky! Colonel Phillips in a correspondence to his superior reported that *"The winter, which so long held off, has set in in earnest; snow three days ago; thermometer four degrees below zero here; for two days it has rained or sleeted."*[21]

Spending just a week or two in Indian Territory Napoleon was assigned to a special detail at the end of January. Of all things he was subpoenaed to testify in a General Court Martial being held at Springfield, Missouri. The Court Martial was being conducted on Lieutenant Colonel Elias Briggs Baldwin, who was in command of the 8th Regiment Missouri Cavalry. He was being charged with the murder of prisoners of war.

These are the chain of events which led to the Court Martial proceedings. As Lieutenant Colonel Baldwin moved his 8th Missouri Cavalry through the town of Huntsville, Arkansas his men detained 9 men thought to be guerrillas who had been harassing Union forces and civilians in the area. In fact several of the men were identified as Confederate soldiers. In the early morning hours of January 10th the 9 detainees were led out into a field and shot without explanation. Eight died in the field and the ninth was presumed dead, but later crawled to a nearby farm for help.

There is a lot of back story here about the Union soldiers seeking revenge for previous attacks on fellow Union soldiers. There had in fact been recent attacks on Union supply wagon trains and executions of Union soldiers in the area. There was a rumor that the nine men shot had ties to these activities. The victims were never brought up on charges so it's hard to say even to this day what they were actually shot for. What's also a mystery is why Napoleon, a mere private and in a totally different regiment, was subpoenaed to testify in this case. As far as I can tell he had no relationship with any of the 9 victims nor anyone in the 8th Missouri Cavalry. The best explanation I can come up with is that he was driving a wagon or acting as an armed escort for one of the wagon trains that the 9 victims were alleged to have attacked, and he was called to describe his attackers. In any case he did go and testify. The result of the Court Martial was that no one was found guilty of the killings and wounding of the survivor. And Lieutenant Colonel Baldwin was acquitted. The incident was dubbed the "Huntsville Massacre" and due to martial law being declared in the area the Court Martial acquittal stood as a legal verdict in the case. After his testimony Napoleon returned to the 6th Kansas Cavalry.

The extreme fighting that had closed out 1862 slowed down for Napoleon and Sam Houston at the beginning of 1863. Most of the major campaigns were being waged further east. As Napoleon scouted in Indian Territory he encountered little action and only the minor skirmish here and there. Sam and his unit were held in reserve north of Little Rock, Arkansas near Prairie Grove. During these lulls in the fighting he spoke of how *"Myself and a few others, when in camp, always held nightly prayer meetings in the groves, praying with and for one another and speaking of the blessed promise of Jesus to the faithful."*[15]

While scouting in Indian Territory in May Napoleon had his horse captured. The company had their horses out grazing, which was standard procedure, and his along with others were captured by the Confederates. The necessity of grazing horses was a vulnerability for cavalrymen. Their horses needed to be fed and as they roamed the country they didn't have the ability to fence them in, so they let them graze the grasslands and prairie around their camp under guard. Obviously guarding them wasn't a for sure way to keep them safe! Riding a government horse for a month or so Napoleon once again purchased and provided his own horse on the 16th of July.

As the two brothers settled into what was for them, a lull in the war, their brother Lewis in Kentucky felt the pressure to pick a side and join the fight. Living in a strong Union section of western Kentucky and only 60 miles from the border with Tennessee, bands of Confederate and guerrilla militias were still operating freely. So Lewis could have joined either side.

The 37 year old father of two was the middle brother between Napoleon and Sam. Standing 5 foot 10 inches tall with blue eyes and a dark complexion he too, supported his family as a farmer. He decided to take up arms with the Union like his brother Napoleon and joined Company A, 48th Regiment Kentucky Mounted Infantry on the 3rd of July 1863. He enlisted at Marion, Kentucky for a term of 1 year and left a wife and several children to fight a war that on the very day he enlisted was raging on the battlefield of Gettysburg, Pennsylvania.

As the 48th Kentucky formed they were granted permission to be a mounted infantry. This designation gave them the ability to have horses and dismount and fight like infantrymen. When the regiment was initially forming they also were without government supplied arms. So Lewis and his comrades provided their own weaponry until a few months later when government weapons arrived.

W | 48 | Ky.

Lewis Walker

Priv; Capt. Hawkins' Co., 48; Reg't Ky. Inf.*

Age 37 years.

Appears on

Company Muster-in Roll

of the organization named above. Roll dated
Princeton Ky, Oct 26, 1863

Muster-in to date Oct 26, 1863

Joined for duty and enrolled:

When July 3, 1863

Where Marion

Period 1 years.

Remarks:

*This organization subsequently became Co. A, 48 Reg't Ky. Inf.

Book mark:

F. B. Neale

(356) Copyist

Lewis Walker's Muster-in Card

As the eastern battle front was raging in early July, the south western front also started to heat up again. Sam found himself headed east in an attempt to relieve besieged Vicksburg, Mississippi. The Union Army, including my great-great grandfather 1st Sergeant John Gunsallus with the 51st Pennsylvania Infantry, had the city surrounded. The Confederate plan was to attack Fort Curtis, a Union fortification at Helena, Arkansas. Located on the Mississippi River upstream from Vicksburg, securing Helena would cutoff Union supplies headed down river to their men attacking Vicksburg. As a matter of fact that's how my great-great grandfather got to Vicksburg with his regiment, by river boat down the Mississippi River right past Fort Curtis.

On the following page is a rough map of the fortifications and initial placement of Union troops at Helena by the U.S. War Department.[21] There were 4 batteries; A, B, C, and D. Battery C and Fort Curtis are directly in front of the square blocks indicating the town of Helena.

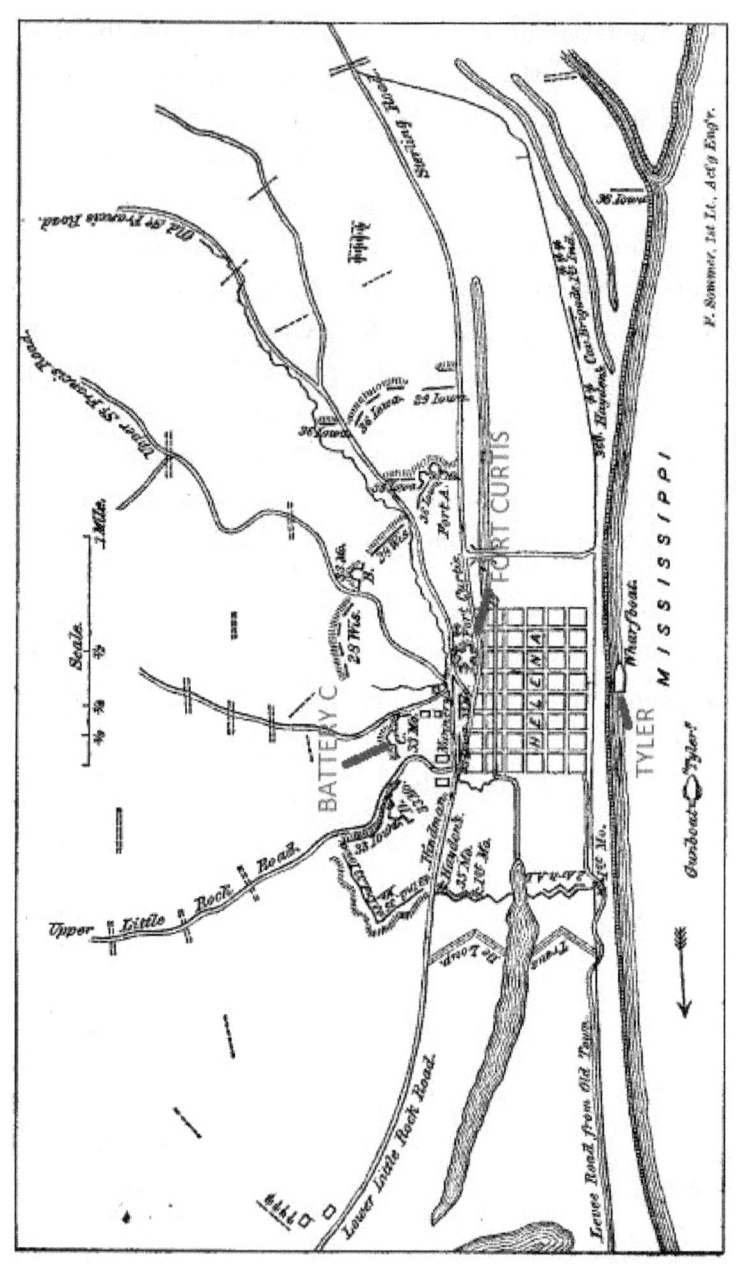

Union held Fort Curtis at Helena, Arkansas[5]

Engaging the enemy on the 4th of July Sam Houston and the Pindall Sharpshooters were part of an attack element on the center of the Union fortification. Fort Curtis was protected by infantry and artillery batteries situated atop of 4 hills surrounding the fort. It also had the naval vessel Tyler stationed on the Mississippi River that protected the water way and provided artillery support. This was one seriously defended fortification and because of that it would be the deadliest day Sam and the Sharpshooters would fight in the war. At midnight Sam Houston as part of Parson's Brigade led the way as it positioned itself for the pending attack. The Sharpshooters were advanced ahead of the brigade to pick off the Union pickets who were to give notice of any pending attack. Eliminating them before they could warn the Union fortification would ensure the Confederates the advantage in a surprise attack. At 3am they attacked, but the fortification had indeed been alerted and Sam's regiment started taking heavy artillery bombardments from the batteries, fort, and the vessel on the Mississippi River.

Union gunboat Tyler on the Mississippi River[5]

Concentrating their attack on Graveyard Hill, which held Union Battery C, Sam and the Sharpshooters led several attacks. Following them were the 9th, 8th, 7th, and 10th, Missouri in that order. At 5am Sam Houston and the Sharpshooters, still leading the way, finally encountered the pickets about ½ mile from the fortifications and fevered skirmishing occurred. Once they had arrived to within musket range of the fortification the Sharpshooters took cover behind anything that would offer protection and delivered heavy fire on the enemy. As they provided supporting fire the rest of the brigade charged Battery C and it was taken.

During the attack Sam's Company Commander, Captain John S. Phillips, was wounded in the neck. The 22 year old captain kept the attack moving even as his men fell around him.

Major General B. M. Prentiss who commanded the Union Army fortifications described Sam Houston's attack;

"For four hours the battle raged furiously, the enemy gaining little, if any, advantage. Now, however, the attack in front became more furious; the enemy covered every hill-top, swarming in every ravine, but seemed to be massing his force more particularly against Battery C. I now signaled the gunboat Tyler, the only one at hand, Lieutenant Commander Pritchett commanding, to open fire in that direction. The enemy (Parson's and McRae's brigades), nothing daunted by the concentrated fire from Fort Curtis, Batteries B, C, and D, the Tyler, and all the infantry I could bring to their support, and led, as I since learned, by Lieutenant General Holmes and Major General Price in person, charged upon Battery C. Twice they were repulsed, but the third time, exhibiting a courage and desperation rarely equaled, they succeeded in driving my small force at the point of bayonet and captured the battery."[21]

After securing Battery C and Graveyard Hill several regiments of Parson's brigade commenced an attack on the town and Fort Curtis. This was the deadliest part of their attack and General Parsons states that half of the men who advanced on the town and fort were killed or captured. The remaining regiments tried to turn the captured artillery pieces on Fort Curtis, the other Batteries, and the Tyler firing from the river, but the artillery would not fire because they had been disabled by the fleeing Union soldiers.

Of the 4 Batteries the only one not directly assaulted was Battery B. And of the three that were assaulted only Battery C was captured. After the failed attempts on the other Batteries and a Union counter attack made on Battery C, Sam and the rest of the Confederate Army withdrew from the battlefield at 10:30am - a Union victory.

View of Helena Battlefield

The picture above is of the battlefield the Confederates advanced on with Hindman Hill in the background. This hill held Union Battery D. The Confederates made 4 attacks on this hill making it up past three levels of rifle pits before being repulsed. I think it gives you a good idea of how high up the Union Batteries were and the great field of fire they had on the advancing Confederates.

Once again Major General Prentiss summarized the conclusion of the battle;

"In the order published to his troops on the 23rd of June ultimo, General Holmes [Commander of Confederate forces fighting at Helena] says, "The invaders have been driven from every point in Arkansas save one – Helena. We go to retake it." I am happy to be able to say that the attempt to haul down the Stars and Stripes, on the 4th of July, was an ignominious failure."[21]

To give you a first-hand account of the battle the following letter is from a Union solder with the 33rd Missouri Infantry which had companies manning all 4 Batteries. His description is of the Confederate force that Sam Houston belonged to attacking him at Fort Curtis, which was behind Battery C.

"Helena, Ark. July 5th 1863

Dear Mother,

I take pen in hand this morning in haste to inform you that I am in excellent health. You will probably have heard before this reaches you that we have a fight here. And most a bloody one it was too. Yesterday morning we were attacked at half past four o'clock by the rebels under Price, Marmaduke and Holmes. We were expecting an attack and as I mentioned to Edna the other day in my letter we were ordered into line every morning before daylight. Yesterday morning I was up at two o'clock and was engaged in delivering some tools to be used in the rifle pits. I remained up the balance of the night. At half past three the Capt ordered me to get the company into line.

Everything was calm and serene and we began to think the rebs had concluded not to attack us. I divided the men into gun squads and scarcely had the men taken their posts ere an officer rode up and ordered us to fire an alarm gun which we did. In ten minutes afterward, the enemy attacked our batteries on the left, almost as the fight opened on the right and center. I think the rebels had their whole force engaged. Our center was headed by two companies of our regiment who were protected by some earthworks in which were planted two brass field pieces. A rebel brigade charged upon this work. They were composed of the 7th, 8th, and 12th Missouri rebel regiments. The ground over which they charged was very broken and the two guns and the infantry in the rifle pits made fearful havoc among them.

The fight by this time was raging fearfully all around the lines. All this time we were standing at our guns. I commanded gun No.6 in Fort Curtis. We loaded first with a shell. The fog was so thick that at the distance of six or seven hundred yards, we could not distinguish our men from the rebels. This was just at sunrise. Gradually as the sun arose, the fog lifted and cleared away and I could see them coming in to flank the battery on the hill opposite us. I asked the Capt if I could give them a fourth *of July salute. He replied to give it to them and thus opened the most murderous fire from our guns that ever men withstood.*

But nothing seemed to daunt the foolhardiness of the rebels; they came on yelling like indians all the time. Our men at the batteries were overpowered and compelled to retreat. They retreated to Fort Curtis. The rebs rushed to the top of the hill and formed a new line. They seemed to think they had gained the day but they were woefully mistaken. While they were forming, we were throwing shot and shell into them that told fearfully. Their colors were posted in a very conspicuous place and time after time they dropped to the ground. Men would rush up and hoist them again but only to be shot down.

As soon as they were formed, they began to advance toward us. They had to cross seven hundred yards of open ground. They seemed as they intended to take us at the bayonet point. They advanced steadily and briskly while six heavy guns from one fort and also several companies of infantry, that had been driven in from the outer works, were mowing them down under this murderous fire. They advanced four hundred yards.

They were so close the day seemed lost in spite of all we could do. At this distance, we poured in a double charge of grape that made them reel and stagger. Their officers waved their swords and tried to urge the men forward, but it was of no use. It was not human to stand it. They broke and began to retreat and such a slaughter was never greater on any battlefield west of the Mississippi. They started up the road and I trained my gun upon it, as also did two other gunners in the fort. We all fired at once and when the smoke cleared away not a man was to be seen within a rod of the place. Dead, dying, and wounded were strewed thickly on the ground. This charge was made down a hill and so perilous was it to retreat that they fell closer to us in a hollow, and the way we did slaughter them was something.

They soon raised a white flag and all of the eighth and tenth Mo rebels regiments surrendered but what lay on the field dead and wounded. We captured one thousand prisoners, two cols., 7 captains, 14 Lts., and guns and accouterments by the card.

I could not give you all the minute details if I were to write two days but will do so in a few days. By eleven o'clock they had retreated and the firing had ceased. And such a looking set of fellows as we were all black with powder as negroes and well we might be for we had fired 103 rounds from our gun during that time. Every one of our company behaved nobly; we are all heroes. Old Pike [County] may well be proud of her representatives here yesterday.

Our Colonel, who was at Pittsburg Landing and Corinth and many other battles of this war says the 33rd are every one heroes. General Salomon says he never saw artillery used more effectively than we did ours yesterday. Not one of us was hurt though the fort is sickening full of balls. The gun carriages [damaged?] but no one was hurt inside the fort. But the enemy were slaughtered.

It was supposed yesterday evening that there were two hundred of their dead on the field, but our men have been burying them since three o'clock yesterday. We find them behind logs and stumps and in hollows. Everyone seems to think that there are at least four hundred of their dead on the field. I have just been over the battlefield and no language can describe its horrors. It was a scene I never shall forget. Men were torn and mutilated in every possible manner. They were all Missourians. Numbers of them surrendered that could easily have escaped. There happened to be a steamboat here at the time and we put six hundred on board of her and started them to Memphis in one hour after the surrender. I suppose you will see an account of it in the papers before I write again. I must close as the mail is ready.

I received letter from Edna this morning.

Our whole loss was 50 killed. 33rd loss 20 killed and some 40 wounded,

So good bye
Henry S. Carroll
Orderly Sergeant, Company D, 33rd Missouri Vols., Inf"[16]

It was a depressing day for the Confederacy. Having been pushed back at Gettysburg the same day and now they were no closer to relieving Vicksburg. And their casualties at Helena were disheartening. The Confederate force that Sam and his regiment belonged to, that attacked the center of the fortification – Parson's Brigade, lost 59 men, with 326 wounded and 368 missing. Sam's regiment alone had 6 killed in action, 19 seriously wounded – 2 mortally, 18 taken prisoner – 2 dying within days from their wounds, 2 missing, and 1 deserter. Most of the severely wounded were taken prisoner because they were left behind on the battlefield with those killed in action. Of these casualties Sam Houston's Company B sustained 1 man killed, 5 seriously wounded – 1 mortally, 18 with minor injuries, 4 taken prisoner – 1 dying days later, and the 1 man that deserted.

The deserter was Private G. N. Richardson who was detailed at the field hospital tending to the wounded. For some reason, probably seeing his comrades being brought in screaming in pain, dying, and missing limbs, he left his post and deserted to the Union.

There are three more interesting notes about the battle and Company B. First, is that of Private Martin Smith. After being captured he was sent to the Union prison at Alton, Illinois. Somehow he was able to escape on the 26th of June 1864. Trying to make his way back to the Sharpshooters he was once again captured in Washington County, Missouri on the 11th of August. He was sent to the Union military prison at Gratiot Street in St. Louis, Missouri and then transferred back to the prison at Alton. But unbelievably he escaped once again on the 5th of December 1864!

Second is that of 1st Lieutenant Jesse M. Strong. Accused of cowardice during the fighting by his company he was acquitted of the charge. With his company and the regiment having lost faith in him, he resigned his commission.

And third is that of the Union men who manned Battery C atop Graveyard Hill. They were fellow Missourians from the 33rd

Missouri. During the attack they had 17 men killed in action, 23 wounded, and 9 missing. These are the official numbers and differ from the first-hand account letter by Sergeant Carroll.

And as for Sam, somehow he escaped Helena, another trial by fire without a scratch.

After being relieved of their scouting duties by several other companies of the 6th Kansas Cavalry Napoleon and Company K arrived back at Fort Scott, Kansas on the 7th of July after almost 6 months of scouting in Indian Territory. Over that time period his company lost more men to disease and illness then to fighting the enemy. They would remain at Fort Scott until mid-August. As Company K recharged, the rest of the 6th Kansas was still active in the fight against the Confederacy in Arkansas.

The companies that relieved Napoleon weren't on scene in Indian Territory long before they engaged the enemy at the Battle of Honey Springs on the 17th of July. I mention this because the battle produced one of the only depictions of the 6th Kansas Cavalry in action that I could find. Although Napoleon wasn't present for the battle I thought it appropriate to include the depiction of the 6th Kansas Cavalry charging into action and on to a Union victory.

The 6th Kansas Cavalry at the Battle of Honey Springs[11]

Lewis was detailed along with the 48th Kentucky to guard the area of Princeton, Kentucky, only a few miles from his wife and kids in Marion. Lewis had never strayed far from the Walker family homestead and was only about 160 miles from his parents in Macon County, Tennessee. The 48th Kentucky Infantry would stay in Princeton until December.

August 4th was a busy day at Fort Scott as Company K joined the rest of the 6th Kansas as they headed south into the Choctaw Nation section of Indian Territory. Napoleon however was detailed under 2nd Lieutenant William Smalley to conduct escort duty. Their mission was to provide an armed escort for a wagon train going from Fort Gibson to Fort Scott and back again. The distance between the forts was 170 miles and would take about 5 days each way. Napoleon and the military escort travelled to Fort Gibson and picked up the wagon train and headed back to Fort Scott.

When they neared Fort Scott around the 1st of August the wagon train continued on to the fort, but Napoleon and two other men were ordered to take several horses to the blacksmith shop, about 2 miles away near Mill Creek, and get them re-shoed. As they rode along Napoleon's horse got spooked throwing him to the ground, breaking and dislocated his left arm and wrist. In extreme pain he was in and out of consciousness. His fellow soldiers carried him to the hospital there at Fort Scott and he was treated by the Assistant Surgeon, Stephen Fairchild. When the wagon train was ready to head back to Fort Gibson Napoleon rode back in an ambulance. Or in Napoleons words *"iwas then wherld into an ambulance and sent to the big mental hospital near ft Gibson."*[25] Once at Fort Gibson he was treated by the Regimental Surgeon, John Redfield.

Napoleon's arm and wrist would bother him for the rest of his life. I'm pretty sure because of the severity of the injury, and him not being able to recover 100 percent, he probably could have received a discharge for not being physically able to perform his duties, but he stayed on to continue fighting.

Meanwhile the rest of Company K and the 6th Kansas had received Intelligence reports placing a Confederate force at the town of Perryville in Indian Territory and using it as a supply depot. After arriving just outside of Perryville on the 23rd it was determined that the main body of Confederate soldiers had vacated the town and only a rear guard remained. With little resistance, the Union force quickly scattered the remaining Confederates and secured what supplies they could. There really wasn't much left because the fleeing Confederates had destroyed most of the supplies, burnt down the town, and spiked the water wells making the town useless. All in all it was a total victory for the Union who sustained no casualties. The Confederates however had 49 casualties. Having secured Perryville the 6th Kansas marched to Fort Gibson where Napoleon rejoined them. From there they scouted in the Cherokee Nation section of Indian Territory until the end of September returning back to Fort Gibson.

Not only were the Walker Brothers currently engaged in fighting but so was their brother-in-law William Harvey Pipkin and soon to be brother-in-law Alfred Harvey Doss. They were the husband and soon to be husband of their younger sisters. Nancy was married to Harvey and Clarissa would marry Alfred after the war. The two had mustered in with the Union side on the same day, the 17th of September 1863 in Glasgow, Kentucky. And they were attached to Company B, 37th Kentucky Infantry.

They were both actively fighting about 130 miles west of where Lewis was in Princeton, Kentucky. The 37th Kentucky Infantry had around 400 men guarding Fort Williams located right at Glasgow, Kentucky where William and Alfred had joined. Not actually encamped within the fort, William and Alfred, along with the rest of their regiment, had set up camp on the outskirts of the fort walls, probably because it was so small. It was really nothing more than built up earthworks. On the 6th of October a raiding party made up of Confederates from the 25th Tennessee realized that they had arrived outside of Glasgow unnoticed. Using the element of surprise on their side they attacked the fort in the early morning, totally surprising the Union men. Capturing it they took their spoils of over 200 horses, saddles, 100 carbines, $9,000 from a local bank, and 142 Union prisoners back into Tennessee. During the attack the Union suffered 9 killed in action and 26 wounded. One of the fatalities was Private William Pipkin who was mortally wounded on the 6th and died from his wounds on the 8th. The 35 year old father of 10 and school teacher wasn't even 3 weeks into his enlistment when he gave his life defending the Union cause. I'm sure the whole Walker family felt a great loss because he was well known to the family. Before marrying Nancy he owned and farmed property next to the Walkers for at least 10 years before moving to Kentucky.

Alfred, who was just a 19 year old private, managed to get away from the Confederate attackers and was not captured. No doubt he was shaken by his first experience in battle and more than likely witnessing the death of William. He regrouped with the remaining men of his regiment and they pulled themselves together to fight another day.

Further west Napoleon and the 6th Kansas marched from Fort Gibson to Fort Smith from the 14th - 19th of November. Fort Smith was now occupied by the Union after the Confederates vacated it. From there Napoleon and Company K left for Little

Rock, Arkansas on the 7th of December as part of an escort for a supply wagon train.

Fort Smith, Arkansas under Union occupation[12]

Lewis and the 48th Kentucky were moved from guard duty at Princeton to guard duty in Russellville, Kentucky on the 1st of December. On the 29th of December his wife gave birth to their daughter Melissa.

Sam Houston finished out the year laying low with Pindall's Sharpshooters at their winter camp, Camp Bragg, located about 17 miles southwest of Camden, Arkansas. On the 17th of December at a local physician's house he lost his 2nd Lieutenant, Albert Stanton, to an illness. He had been battling the effects of the illness for the past year, but stayed for the most part fighting with his men. He was only 23 years old.

1864

Napoleon escorted the supply wagon train safely to Little Rock, and then he and Company K returned to Fort Smith on the 13th of January. It was a hard journey and the men encountered freezing temperatures, which fell near zero degrees. A cold front had blanketed the area and being out in these extreme elements could be deadly. Wintering out the next month they remained at the fort performing scouting and picket duties. On the 17th of February they were ordered 40 miles away to Roseville, Arkansas where the company remained until the 26th of March. Roseville was an important Union river crossing and landing on the Arkansas River. Supplies and ammunition were brought up the river and unloaded there, making it strategically important to the Union Army.

Beginning on the 31st of March the Union Army implemented a plan to take military control over the entire states of Arkansas, Louisiana, and Texas. Up until this point they were pretty much only in control of the forts they held at Fort Smith, Pine Bluff, Helena, and Little Rock. Operating between these safe havens the Confederate Army and guerrilla militias were a deadly threat.

The Union plan would however once again pit Napoleon and Sam Houston's army divisions against each other.

Back in Kentucky Lewis was just getting back to his unit after taking leave from the 31st of March to the 15th of April. While he was away the 48th Kentucky were moved on the 6th of April. The regiment was split up and each company was assigned a section of the Louisville & Nashville Railroad. His company was now assigned 12 miles away from their previous location to guard the rail station at Elizabethtown, Kentucky. Lewis more than likely rode the same train he was now guarding when he went on leave because the Louisville and Nashville line ran through Marion, Russellville, and Elizabethtown.

As his company was moving they were attacked by guerrillas at Nolin Station, one stop before their final destination. One man from Company A was wounded in the face, and the guerrilla's sustained 1 man and 2 horses captured. Guarding the railroads was dangerous work. The Confederates were constantly trying to destroy it in order to disrupt Union supply trains and to also pillage what was on the trains.

Now stationed just 50 miles north of where his brother-in-law William Pipkin was killed at Glasgow, the Confederates and guerrilla militias operated freely in the area. This must have weighed heavily on Lewis as he worried about his family 150 miles to the west back in Marion County. Although a little out of the way for any major military activity there were several skirmishes back home and Confederate guerrillas operated freely in the area.

The spring weather of April would bring Napoleon and Sam Houston to battle on the same day, but on different battlefields. In early April Napoleon and the 6th Kansas were preparing for the Battle of Prairie D'Ane in Arkansas and Sam Houston and his Sharpshooters were preparing for the Battle of Pleasant Hill, Louisiana.

Prairie D'Ane was a very important strategic crossroad for both sides. After the Union took control of Little Rock in 1863, the Confederate capital in Arkansas, they had moved it to Washington, Arkansas. If the vital crossroad at Prairie D'Ane were to fall into Union hands it would leave the new Confederate capital and the important city of Camden exposed.

While at their encampment at Roseville, the 6th Kansas split; Companies A, C, G, K, and M would head south for Prairie D'Ane and the remainder would protect the encampment and provide wagon train escort duty. The companies providing escort duty, Companies D, E, I and L suffered 14 men killed in action and 1 wounded while escorting a supply wagon train on the 4th and 5th of April. They were attacked by a superior number of Confederates made up of the 13th Texas Cavalry. The losses protecting the encampment at Roseville and conducting escort duties over this two day period was one of the worse the 6th had seen since entering the war.

One of the men killed during these encounters on the 5th was Assistant Surgeon Stephen Fairchild. If you remember he was the surgeon who treated Napoleon's broken arm and wrist at Fort Scott.

Now headed south Napoleon and the other companies would encounter more guerrilla attacks along with heavy fortifications and barricades on their way to Prairie D'Ane. By the 4th Napoleon and Companies A, C, G, K, and M had crossed the Little Missouri River by pontoon bridge and joined with a larger Union force, engaging the enemy on the 10th. As the battle was waging the Companies of the 6th Kansas were sent around towards Washington, Arkansas in a ploy to draw the main Confederate concentration from Prairie D'Ane. The fighting continued over the next several days as both sides tried to position themselves for the best advantage in a head to head fight. As the 6th Kansas acted as a diversion to the west the remaining Union force headed toward the key town of Camden and easily secured it. By the 13th Napoleon and Company K had completed their diversion and by the 16th had re-joined the Union Army at Camden. A Union victory, they now held control of Prairie D'Ane and Camden. Casualties were considered light and estimates are that the Union sustained 100 men killed or wounded and the Confederates 50 men.

At the same time about 150 miles south in Pleasant Hill, Louisiana Sam Houston and the Sharpshooters were engaged in battle. Arriving late in the day on the 8th they had just missed the Battle of Mansfield, a Confederate victory. During the battle the Confederates had pushed back an outnumbered Union force several miles to Pleasant Hill until it was reinforced and the Confederates held their position. Throughout the night both sides received reinforcements as regiments like Sam Houston's moved in to join the fight.

The town of Pleasant Hill consisted of only about 12 to 15 houses concentrated in a clearing of Pine and scrub-Oak brush. The two armies felt each other out and by 1pm on the 9th were engaging in random skirmishes until around 5 pm when the Confederates launched a full scale attack.

The map on the following page from the United States War Department[21] shows the battle map of the Battle of Pleasant Hill at 5pm when the fighting began. If you look at the top of the map you will see Parson's Division in which Sam Houston belonged.

As Sam Houston charged forward with the rest of Parson's Division they were headed straight for the Unions 30th Maine and 162nd, 165th, and 173rd New York Infantries. The following description of Sam attacking them is from Colonel Francis Fessenden of the 30th Maine;

"Shortly after the skirmishers of the brigade in the woods were driven in, and had not yet joined the battalion when the enemy appeared in the edge of the woods, in front and beyond the left of the line. They advanced rapidly in two lines obliquely upon the left and across the front of the brigade, extending well toward the right. They advanced at a charging pace, delivering a very heavy fire as they advanced.

Two companies of the Thirtieth Maine deployed in the ditch, one in front of that regiment and the other between that and the One Hundred and Sixty-Second New York Volunteers, opened a sharp fire upon the enemy, but without checking them in the least. These companies fell back, one upon its own regiment and another toward the One Hundred and Sixty-Second New York Volunteers. The enemy charged swiftly from the slope and commenced crossing the ditch, striking at some of the skirmishers in the ditch with the butts of their muskets. So rapidly did they advance that Lieutenant-Colonel Blanchard, [162nd NY] who had gone to the front of his regiment to the ditch for purpose of seeing the position of the enemy, had not time to place himself behind his regiment before the brigade line commenced retiring in confusion.

The regiments fell back beginning with the One Hundred and Sixty-Fifth New York Volunteers on the right, followed by the One Hundred and Sixty-Second New York Volunteers on the center and the One Hundred and Seventy-Third New York Volunteers next, the regiments delivering their fire as they fell back in disorder to the rear."[21]

And this is how Sam's Brigadier General Parson's described his men in action;

"My sharpshooters, under Major Pindall, were hotly engaged with the enemy……I deem it due to the officers and soldiers of my command to state that this charge of nearly 700 yards over open ground, and against two lines of the enemy drawn up and protected in the most favorable positions, was the most brilliant feat that I have witnessed during the present war."[21]

The map on the following page from the United States War Department[21] shows the battle map of the Battle of Pleasant Hill at 5:45pm, and how far Sam Houston and Parson's Division advanced in just 45 minutes. You can see Parson's Division towards the middle of the map, well past where the Union front lines were previously.

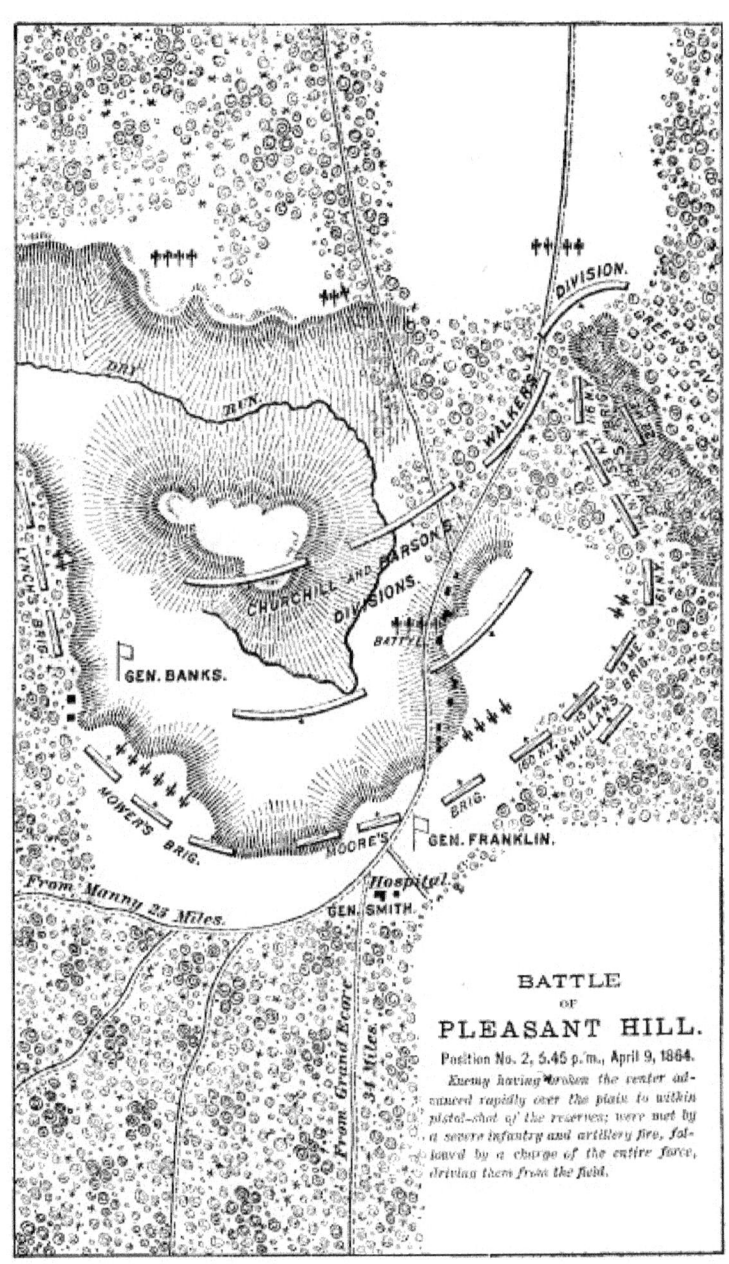

The attack was successful and Sam Houston and the Sharpshooters, along with other elements, broke through the first line of Union positions. The broken Union lines eventually regrouped and halted the Confederate advance and were saved from a rout only because of darkness. The fierce fighting lasted about 2 hours. After sustaining heavy casualties over the past two days the Union Army fell back at about 1am on the morning of the 10th, leaving Pleasant Hill in Confederate control. Losses for the Union were 150 men killed in action, 844 wounded, and 375 missing. The Confederates lost 1,200 men killed or wounded with 426 captured. Of these figures Parson's Division sustained 32 killed in action, 235 wounded, and 51 missing. Of those, Sam Houston's Sharpshooters had 11 men wounded – 1 mortally. After the battle Private Henry Manesy was selected by Sam Houston and Company B for the Confederate Roll of Honor for distinguishing himself above and beyond the call of duty during the battle.

After securing Camden the split up companies of the 6th Kansas regrouped at Camden. In preparation for a long trip back to Little Rock Napoleon's Company K, along with several other companies were detailed to secure stored corn. The Union Army was low on food and the corn was vital to sustaining their planned march north. However, the corn was located back towards the strategic crossroads of Prairie D'Ane near White Oak Creek. On the 18th Napoleon made it to the corn and it was loaded on wagons. The loaded wagon train then headed back towards Camden and the awaiting Union Army. After going only 8 miles the slow moving wagon train was attacked by Confederates from the front and the rear. Abandoning their wagons the Union men headed for a defensive position located in a nearby swamp. Covering their retreat were members of the all black 1st Kansas Colored Infantry.

Repelling the first two attacks the former slaves of the 1st Kansas held their own as the rest of the Union men fell back to the swamp. On the third Confederate assault the 1st Kansas was overrun. Refusing to take the wounded black solders of the 1st Kansas prisoners the Confederates instead brutally killed, scalped, and stripped them. Not wanting to engage the remaining Union contingent well protected in the swamp the Confederates returned to their spoils of corn. Continuing their retreat the Union men returned empty handed back to Camden. In all the 1st Kansas lost nearly half of the men it had sent to assist the wagon train. The total Union losses were 301 casualties, 198 wagons, and all the corn lost. Napoleon's Company K reported Private Nathan Cunningham as missing in action and Private H. Gable severely wounded and captured. Company D lost Private Columbus Goodman, killed in action and Lieutenant Robert Henderson was wounded. The Confederates reported 114 casualties.

Once again, like what happened at Roseville, the loss of this supply wagon train proved the dire need for the Union to secure the entire state in order to protect its supply columns. The ability of the Union Army to operate in these southern states depended on military supremacy.

Without the much needed corn to nourish them on their journey, Napoleon and the 6th Kansas departed Camden and headed north towards the safety of Little Rock. At the same time Sam Houston and the Sharpshooters were headed north from Pleasant Hill to intercept them. Fresh off of a decided victory Sam Houston would cover over 200 miles trying to catch his brother before he reached Little Rock.

The morning of the 29th of April was rainy as the long Union Army column headed north. Napoleon and Company K, along with Company C, were providing the rear guard support for the Union column. At 10am scouting elements of Sam Houston and the Confederates clashed in a sharp skirmish with Napoleon and Company K and C as the main Union body crossed the Ouachita River. Company K sustained 2 men missing and Company C had Private E. Gray wounded.

Now converging on the area Sam Houston and Parson's Division joined other Confederate divisions, pausing to formulate a plan of attack. As they paused they tried to build fires to dry themselves and were ordered to hurriedly cook 3 days' worth of rations for the impending fight and possible continued chase. The 30th began with heavy downpours of rain, rain that had been falling for several days. This made transiting tough for both sides. Artillery and wagons were slowing everyone down as they were sucked into the wet ground, which quickly turned to mud. As Sam Houston and the rest of Parson's Division were trying to rest, cook, and dry out, volleys of gunfire erupted to their front at around 8am. Hearing the gunfire the division moved forward.

Confederate scouts had once again engaged Napoleon and the Union Army. They had arrived at their next river crossing on the Saline River. Finding the river flooded and overflowing its banks from all the rain, there was no way to cross. But they had a pontoon bridge with them and started to install it, although the fast moving water exceeded its operating limits. As they were attempting to install the bridge the infantry began to set up a defensive position in anticipation of the Confederates, who were right on their heels. Successfully completing the bridge they commenced moving over 5,000 men along with hundreds of wagons, mules, horses, and Union civilians. As they moved their assets to the other side of the river, Sam Houston and the Confederates attacked. The weather was hampering the Union crossing but it was also slowing the Confederates advance as they tried to fight in the boggy, swampy areas leading up to the crossing.

Fierce fighting broke out as the two armies fought in pouring rain and mud. Attacking as they arrived, Sam Houston and the Sharpshooters were among the first to engage his brother and the dug in Union Army. Sam and his unit were detailed as infantry on the right flank. But they lacked any type of coordinated attack and became disorganized in the swamp. Thus, the Confederates made no headway. By 3pm Napoleon and the Union Army had made it to the other side of the Saline River and destroyed the pontoon bridge, protecting their escape. Safe on the other side, they found that their wagons were bogging down and getting stuck in the mud. In order to prevent the Confederates from getting their hands on the supplies the Union men were ordered to destroy anything that could not be moved. This included the regimental records of the 6th Kansas. Sam Houston and the Confederates were so exhausted from the fighting in the bad weather they didn't try to cross the river and held their position.

Captain John Whiteford of the Union's 1st Arkansas Infantry described the battle in a letter to his wife;

"The infantry were in the rear to protect the train, and fight the rebels, while the balance of the army were crossing on the pontoon. It was a regular infantry fight. The rebels had four pieces of artillery in making the attack on us, but the Second Kansas Colored Volunteers captured that after the third charge, and then we had an even show. They massed their infantry on us and charged fiercely, but it was no go. Our regiment distinguished itself. The dead rebels were thick over the ground. As we drove them back one man, by my side, was shot, and the bushes and sapplings were cutting down in front of me and bark and dirt thrown in my face, but no ball touched me. Thanks to God, who saw fit to spare my life awhile longer. The musketry was fiercer and more constant than at Prairie Grove. We fought all day on swampy land. The night before we were up all night in the rain in line of battle, and during the fight we were up to our knees in water, and when we had drove the enemy back we had to march on return four miles through mud knee deep. Union families from Camden had to leave their carriages in the mud, and carry their children to the bridge. Men even dropped down in the confusion and wagons pass over them, it raining all the time. When we got across the

bridge we had three miles more of such mud. Such a sight of women and children crying, and horses and mules dying, and wagons abandoned, I never saw. The rebels came to the river after we had crossed, but too late to do us any damage. We had destroyed the bridge that night, and all the wagons except one to each brigade."[17]

And a Confederate soldier from the division that Sam Houston belonged described the aftermath and having to bury the dead;

"After the battle a detail of men were employed in burying the dead. Armed with shovel, pick ax and spade they proceeded along the road to complete this mournful task which the enemy was unable to accomplish. The ground was thickly strewn with ghostly, mangled forms. It was almost too horrible for human endurance. No conception of the imagination, no power of human language could do justice to such a horrible scene."[18]

The Battle of Jenkins Ferry is considered one of the more bloody battles of the Civil War west of the Mississippi River. The Confederates suffered over 1,000 casualties and the Union 700 casualties. Sam Houston's regiment sustained 4 wounded, 1 coming from his company – Sergeant W. B. Stiles who was severely wounded in the side. And Napoleon's Company K had one man taken prisoner. Their casualties were light because they were detailed to guard the river crossing and escort the wagon train after they crossed, while the infantry was dug in repelling the majority of the attack.

And so the two Walker Brothers one again walked off the battlefield, probably never knowing that each other was there and how close they came to possibly killing each other.

On the 3rd of May Napoleon and the 6th Kansas Cavalry made it safely to Little Rock. Meanwhile Sam Houston and the 9th Missouri Sharpshooters moved south towards Louisiana. Unknown to both of them, this would be the last major engagement either of the two brothers would be involved in.

Heading south, Sam Houston and the sharpshooters stopped on the Arkansas and Louisiana border in the little town of Three Creeks, Arkansas, named so for the three creeks that converge there. He said that while he was there we *"Had one of the most wonderful revivals it has ever been my privilege to witness."*[15] It was led by the Sharpshooter's Chaplain, George W. Smith and a Baptist Minister by the name of Painter. Sam states that *"Four Hundred converts were baptized upon profession of their faith in Christ."*[15] Sounds like the three creeks got a good workout that day! Leaving Three Creeks Sam's regiment continued on south and eventually halted in Shreveport, Louisiana where they guarded the city.

Napoleon and the 6th Kansas, after regrouping and resupplying the regiment, headed back across Arkansas to Fort Smith, arriving there on the 16th of May. But the war was far from being over for the 6th Kansas Cavalry, Napoleon, and Company K. On the 2nd of June Napoleon's Company Commander, Captain John Rogers, was killed in a skirmish near Fort Scott as they performed scouting duties.

On the 1st of July Napoleon was relieved of duty as the wagoner and reassigned back to duty as a mounted cavalryman and private. Probably having mixed emotions he had been the wagoner pretty much since joining. But always bringing up the rear and a pretty tempting target for the enemy the job had its dangers. Now riding up in formation he would be in every fight.

Battling the enemy on the 15th Corporal William Hood of Company K was killed in a skirmish near Carthage, Missouri. The war was taking its toll on the 6th Cavalry as they escorted and scouted in the enemy infested areas between their safe havens of forts. But the deadliest engagement the 6th Kansas would experience throughout the war occurred on the 27th of July.

Splitting in half as they did so many times before, the 6th Kansas Cavalry left 4 companies about 6 miles from Fort Smith on outpost duty and Napoleon and the remaining companies where sent out scouting. On the morning of the 27th the 4 companies, totaling about 200 men, on outpost duty were grazing their horses on Mazzard Prairie. At 6am a force of over 1,000 Confederate Cavalrymen, consisting of Texans and Choctaw Indians, attacked. The unsuspecting men of the 6th Kansas had their horses driven away and had to fight without them. Outnumbered and surprised the 4 companies were overtaken. The 6th Kansas lost 15 men killed in action, 15 wounded, and 44 taken prisoner. The men that evaded the enemy hid in the dense underbrush until the Confederates had left the area. After making off with all the 6th Kansas's horses, supplies, and prisoners, the Confederates had a unanimous victory only losing 7 men killed in action and 26 wounded.

Continuing on with their duties the remaining companies of the 6th Kansas stayed in the vicinity of Fort Smith. And just a few miles away near Van Burren, Arkansas on the 12th of August Private William Harris of Company K was killed in a skirmish.

Napoleon was detailed once again as an armed escort for a wagon train to Fort Scott. Leaving on the 14th of August the 200 mile trip each way would take him 17 days to complete. Navigating the dangerous guerrilla infested areas of Indian Territory, Arkansas, and south western Missouri, he arrived back safely on the 31st.

Back in Kentucky, Lewis and the 48th Kentucky were gearing up for a busy August and reassigned on the 13th about 100 miles to the west at Calhoun, Kentucky. Now only 50 miles from his wife and kids he must have felt better. Briefly held by Confederate Guerrillas in 1862 Calhoun and its valuable saw and flour mills had been in Union control since they chased the Confederates out in 1862.

Although designated as a mounted infantry regiment the 48th had until this point been used primarily as stationary infantry. But that was to change. On the 19th of August they were mounted and on the move chasing down Confederate General Adam Johnson. After General Johnson was wounded and captured at Grubbs Crossroads, Lewis and the 48th Kentucky scouted for guerrillas operating in counties bordering the Cumberland River, just across the border in Tennessee.

Now fighting back near his boyhood home in Tennessee he must have had mixed feelings fighting against people he more than likely grew up with. Lewis operated in this area until his enlistment was up on the 17th of December. He was discharged at nearby Bowling Green, Kentucky and only had to travel 120 miles to get back home to his wife and kids. And once again he probably took the Louisville and Nashville railroad. His leave back in March must have been enjoyable because he arrived home just in time for the birth of his daughter Narcisie on the 29th of December.

Leaving the 48th Kentucky must have been very conflicting for Lewis. The war was still raging in late 1864 and he undoubtedly wanted to participate or he wouldn't have joined. But he also had a family and farm that needed taken care of. Plus the area he lived in was always susceptible to Confederate Army, Militia, and Guerrilla activity. Although the state was officially in Union control these roving Confederates made every day at home potentially dangerous, especially for an ex-Union soldier.

Sam Houston closed out 1864 in Shreveport, Louisiana which was now the Confederate capital of Louisiana. He and the rest of the 9th Missouri Sharpshooters were posted at Fort Albert Sidney Johnston, which was the headquarters for the Confederates operating in the Trans-Mississippi Department. The fort sat atop a ridge on the northwest side of the city and offered great protection. As Sam waited the war out in Shreveport his wife was safely settling into to life in Texas 135 miles away. Sam must have gotten a chance to get back to visit with her earlier in the year because she gave birth to their son William on the 21st of October.

As 1864 came to a close most of the major fighting was being conducted on the east coast in Virginia and the Carolinas. And Union forces held control of the majority of Missouri, Arkansas, and half of Louisiana. The only contested parts of Arkansas were the south eastern corner where Napoleon was fighting. And the half of Louisiana that was still in Confederate control was where Sam Houston was fighting.

1865

In January Napoleon was once again sent on a special detail, this time it was to Spadra Bluff, Arkansas. Located about 60 miles east of Fort Smith, Spadra Bluff was a small river port used by the Union Army. Napoleon's mission was to guard government property there. Although Spadra Bluff held no military facilities it was on a wide part of the Arkansas River that was great for off-loading and on-loading supplies. The government equipment he was guarding was more than likely barges or steamers used to transit the river carrying supplies, equipment, and men.

With more and more decisive battles being won by the Union at the beginning of 1865 the Confederacy was crumbling, but they were still putting up a fight. Napoleon still encountered skirmishes with the enemy and the 6th Kansas had a man from Company L killed in action near Fort Smith on the 12th of February. The regiment moved to De Valls Bluff near Little Rock in late February and a man from Company I was wounded on the 18th of March. On the same day Napoleon was mustered out of Company K as the regiment released its men who had enlisted for 3 years back in March of 1862. Like his brother Lewis, Napoleon must have been conflicted about leaving his regiment. The bond he had made with his fellow comrades was one only a service member can relate to. Fighting and enduring the hardships of living off the land with his fellow cavalrymen was a bond that would last a lifetime. And at this point in his life they were like family to him. But after 3 years of this extremely hard lifestyle he must have wanted to move on with his life. And who could blame him? The war in his eyes was appearing to wind down. Why not leave when he had the chance. Making his way back to Kansas he traveled through dangerous areas still harassed by Confederates, as evidenced by the previously mentioned casualties.

Sam Houston was seeing little action at Fort Johnston. Most of the Confederate units fighting in the south were protecting valuable cities or fighting in Alabama. Though life at the fort may have been without fighting, it wasn't without death. Disease and chronic diarrhea kept the Confederate hospital there busy and resulted in numerous deaths.

Then on the 1st of April the capital of the Confederacy, Richmond, Virginia fell. The President of the Confederate States, Jefferson Davis fled Richmond after it fell with the intent of reaching Shreveport and rallying the Confederacy, but he never made it. He was captured on his way south through Georgia. Shortly after the fall of Richmond General Robert E. Lee surrendered his army in Virginia on the 9th. And on the 26th the Army of Tennessee and its 90,000 men surrendered, a crimpling blow to the Confederacy. Not long afterwards on the 9th of May President Johnson declared the war over. But Sam Houston and the Trans-Mississippi Department at Fort

Johnston would not surrender until the 26th of May, holding out some final hope for their cause.

Finally surrendering, Sam *"stacked his arms"*[15] there at Fort Johnston with the rest of his comrades. He had made it through the war without ever *"feeling the sting of a bullet and during [the war] enjoyed very good health."*[15] Now considered a prisoner he had to swear allegiance to the United States before being released. With the war and his enlistment over he then started his journey home to his wife and baby in Red River, Texas.

On the 9th of June at 4pm the bulk of the 9th Missouri Sharpshooters, along with members of other units and family members, were loaded on the steamer Kentucky. Shortly after getting underway and heading north on the Red River, the steamer struck a submerged cypress stump. Rather than stop for repairs or find other transports for the Confederates, the federal officer responsible for the transport continued on without taking any corrective action. That same evening, around 11pm while most of the passengers were asleep, the boat quivered and began filling with water. Those on deck urgently attempted to get the boat tied up to the river bank, but it snapped it's mooring line and spun out into the river! Within minutes the Kentucky was half submerged and sinking in the river. While an exact death toll was never determined, only about 400 of the approximately 690 passengers and crew were rescued or found alive the next morning.

Providentially, Sam and several others had split off from their regiment as they all headed their separate ways. So they were spared this parting shot from the hell they had fought so hard to survive. Ironically, doggedly, after surviving 3 years of warfare, poor food, disease, and exposure to the elements, the surviving men of the 9th Missouri Sharpshooters dried themselves on the banks of the Red River. They buried their comrades who just hours before must have been joyous at finally starting for home and loved ones.

The war was over.

After the war

Arriving back home in Red River, Texas Sam Houston took up his passion for preaching the good Word of the Lord and farming. In June of 1866 he joined the Salem Baptist Church which licensed him to become a preacher. The following year he was ordained as a Baptist Minister. He remained with the Salem Baptist Church for 26 years preaching principally in Red River, but also in Titus and Bowie Counties.

In November of 1890 he fell from a wagon and broke his hip and left wrist. This didn't slow Sam Houston down and he continued to preach the good Word *"In the waste places, by-ways, and hedges."*[15] At about this time he moved his family to Abbott, Texas which is just north of Waco.

As Sam's age and ailments caught up with him he applied for a Civil War Veteran's Pension through the state of Texas at the age of 69, claiming he was unable to support himself anymore. And on the 3rd of November 1899, about 4 months after he applied, his pension was granted for $22 a month[10]. It's interesting to note that on his application he had two witnesses that he brought to testify of his Confederate service. The first was an Arthur J.G. Smith. Serving with Sam in the 9th Sharpshooters he was in Company D. The second was J. T.

Dunlap. He served in the 3rd Battery Missouri Light Artillery. They were assigned with the 9th Sharpshooters to provide artillery support during the war and were with them at their darkest days at the Battle of Helena, and stationed with them at Fort Johnston in Shreveport. Since Sam's 9th Sharpshooters didn't have artillery that's probably an artillery piece from J.T. Dunlap's 3rd Battery that Sam is standing in front of in the picture on the front cover of this book.

Because these men were not from Sam's company I assume they knew each other through the many religious get-togethers that were such an integral part of Sam's life while in the army.

It seems like with most men and women who serve their country in battle and peace time, these men became friends who stayed in touch. And almost 35 years after being discharged they met again in a lawyer's office to once again take care of Confederate business.

Pensions were entirely different between Confederate and Union soldiers. Union soldiers and their widows could file for an invalid or widow pension right away. And in the 1890's a federal law was passed to offer pensions to all Union veterans. Confederate veterans on the other hand could only file through the state they lived in or fought for. And that wasn't until the early 1890's when southern states started to pass laws for their own veteran pensions. These Confederate pensions were, however, less than their Union counterparts and one of the many downfalls of being on the losing side.

Sam Houston Walker's Confederate Pension Application

Sam Houston lived another 10 years after receiving his pension, until the 21st of April 1910. He died in Calhoun County, Texas and was buried there at the Bendewald Farm Cemetery. He left behind his wife and six children, his first child having died as an infant. His decedents still live in Calhoun County and the Walker name is still well known there.

Originally buried on a bluff at the Bendewald family cemetery he was only a few yards from the bay. It was a beautiful and peaceful place to be buried. But over the years the bluff started to erode away and several headstones fell in the water. Sam's 19th century great grandchildren feared his grave and headstone would also fall into the bay, so an attempt was made to exhume his body but nothing was found. Nature had obviously run its course and as the saying goes, and I think Sam would appreciate, "ashes to ashes, dust to dust." His family had his grave marker renewed and moved it to the cemetery in Seadrift, Texas a few miles away. I have been to this cemetery and his grave numerous times. He is, again, in a peaceful setting surrounded by family.

In the author section at the end of this book I have included a picture of myself at his grave site that was taken on Memorial Day 2017. After I placed the Confederate Battle Flag on his grave I wondered how long it would last until it was taken down. Unfortunately, political correctness today frowns upon the Confederate flag as if history should be rewritten to exclude anything that makes us uncomfortable. But it still waves and serves as a reminder of an American man who offered his very life for a cause he believed in.

Reverend Samuel Houston Walker

Lewis with his second wife and 4 of their children

Lewis returned to Marion, Kentucky and picked up where he had left off as a farmer. His first wife Mary Goober passed away in 1874. Soon after, at the age of 49, he married again to another Mary, 22 year old Mary Belt. He went on to have a total of 9 children. In 1887 he applied for a veteran's pension. After he passed, his widow applied for his pension and after she passed one of his minor children applied for his benefits. So, Lewis ended up getting a lot of financial mileage out of his one year of service! Passing away on the 17th of May 1896 he is buried with his second wife Mary Belt there in Marion, Kentucky.

After being discharged from the Army in Arkansas, Napoleon went back to Kansas and married 17 year old Mary Bunch. He lived with Mary and her parents on their farm in Paris, Kansas for several years before moving back to Jasper, Missouri in 1868 where he had been working before the war. In 1890 he moved back to his old war time stomping grounds, residing just outside of Fort Gibson in Tahlequah, Indian Territory. He stayed here with his family until mid-1890 when he moved 40 miles east, just across the state line, to Evansville, Arkansas.

Soon after being discharge Napoleon applied for an invalid veteran's pension in September of 1865. His left arm and wrist never healed properly and his arm became deformed and virtually useless. He was granted an invalid pension of $4 a month. Over the years he continued to apply for increases because of his failing arm. He is noted as saying in one of his increase requests that he could only do half a day's work because of it. And in 1890 it was increased to $12 and in 1907 to $20.

I have attached Napoleon's Muster Out Card because I think it shows a few interesting things. First, he was charged $29 for clothing issued to him. Second, it shows that the army was charging him $1 for a box of carbine ammunition he was taking with him when he separated. Third, the last time he was paid was the end of June 1864. That's over 9 months from the time he was discharged and his account settled! And finally, it shows that he was still due his full $100 bounty – minus his clothing and ammunition cost. So with all his back pay and the remainder of his bounty, Napoleon was leaving the army with a lot of money!

He and Mary had 13 children over the course of their long marriage. Napoleon died on the 11th of December 1909 in Arkansas. After his death Mary applied, and was granted, his veteran's benefits. He must have been proud of his service with Company K and the 6th Kansas, as his family had it inscribed on his tombstone. Mary passed away in 1926 and is resting next to him.

```
W | 6 Cav. | Kans.

            Napoleon B. Walker
      Priv    , Co. K ,  6 Reg't Kansas Cav.

Age  31  years.
Appears on a
        Detachment Muster-out Roll
of the organization named above.  Roll dated
  Ft Halls Bluff, Ark , Mch 22, 1865 .
Muster-out to date        Mch 18, 1865 .
Last paid to              June 30, 1864 .

Clothing account:
Last settled June 30, 1864; drawn since $ 29 76/100
Due soldier $......100; due U.S. $......100
Am't for cloth'g in kind or money adv'd $......100

Due U.S. for arms, equipments, &c., $...... 1 00/100
Bounty paid $......100; due $. 150 100
Valuation of horse, $............100
Valuation of horse equipments, $......100
Remarks: Stp for 1 Cart Card Box "100
Mustered out by reason of expi-
ration of term of service under
War Dept Cir 41 of 1864

Book mark:

                          Wilson
  (349)                    Copyist.
```

Napoleon Bonaparte Walker's Muster Out Card

Napoleon Bonaparte Walker's tombstone[6]

The brothers' sister, Nancy, applied for and was granted a widow's pension from the federal government in November of 1865 for the loss of her husband William Pipkin. She was awarded $22 per month. This amount was $8 for being a widow and $2 for each child, of her 7 children, who were under the age of 16 years of age. Nancy moved back to Lafayette in Macon County, Tennessee near her parents after the war. Then to Franklin, Illinois where she died in 1872.

Their sister Clarissa's soon-to-be husband, Alfred Dodd, made it through the war. After the fight at Glasgow that claimed his future brother-in-law he continued on with Company B operating in Kentucky and into southwest Virginia. He was mustered out on the 29th of December 1864 in Louisville, Kentucky when his enlistment was up and his company disbanded. He and Clarissa married in 1876 and he died on the 8th of June 1889, and is laid to rest along with Clarissa at the Underwood Cemetery in Macon County, Tennessee.

I'm speculating here, but I don't think that Sam Houston and Napoleon knew at the time that they were fighting against each other at various engagements during the war. But I'm sure they knew they were fighting on opposite sides. Each would have stayed in contact with their parents and other siblings and would have learned who sided with whom. Certainly, their close calls became evident after the war as every skirmish and battle was dissected and written about. The fact is, the 6th Kansas Cavalry and Pindall's Sharpshooters fought in the same area and bumped heads on several occasions. Knowing what regiment each other was in would have definitely alerted them to the fact that they had opposed each other on the battlefield.

They must have been close before the war since they left home, travelling nearly 600 miles together, and then working in Missouri on farms near each other. But after the war, when they settled down and started their own families they seem to have gone their separate ways. Neither one named a child after the other, which was common during that time period when you had really big families. And they had plenty of opportunities, Napoleon had 13 children and Sam Houston 7. They did however name several of their children after their parents and other siblings. It's also interesting that they ended up spending most of their post war years only a couple hundred miles from each other. But Sam Houston never mentions leaving the state of Texas after returning from the war and there is no record of Napoleon traveling to Texas. Of course they could have corresponded by mail, but from what I can gather the war divided them for the rest of their lives.

In the end, the three brothers made it through the Civil War without killing each other! And went on to live productive lives. One could not ask, nor imagine a more American story…

In closing

It was really fun compiling information on the Walker family for this book and have my daily research take me through the dynamic lives of these three men and their siblings. In my research I went down so many rabbit holes thinking I had a lead on a certain aspect of the book or a family member, only to have it crumble away as the facts played out differently than I anticipated. But that's the fun of researching!

If you have the time I would encourage you to research your family and see what surprises you may uncover. To start, have a look at my references. Web based search sites Ancestry.com and Fold3.com are a must. Ancestry.com lets you build family trees, and this makes it so much easier to follow your ancestors back through the generations. Believe me, as you start to go back even just one generation, it starts to get confusing. Plus Ancestry.com has census, death, birth, marriage, and some military documents that are so valuable for verifying you have the correct family member. As an example, how many Napoleon Bonaparte Walkers do you think would have fought in the Civil War? I thought with a name like that there could only be one. Well Fold3.com, which specializes in military records, came back with over 13,000 records! There were Napoleon Bonaparte Walkers who fought for Alabama, New

York, Illinois, and several other states. Clearly not the ones I was looking for. And finding the right one is obviously important. The best way I found to verify my Walkers were through marriage licenses, and death certificates. Death certificates usually have the individual's parents' names on them, which is a sure lock that you have the correct person. I also find that more recent marriage records are also a great help. Older ones usually just have the bride and groom's names with no parents mentioned.

If you run into multiple soldiers with the same name and in similar regiments, try this; first determine who their spouse is, then search the pension records on each person that is in your pool of possible candidates. If the spouse matches, you have your man.

Confederate pensions can be a little more difficult because they were controlled by each individual state, unlike the Union pensions that were all handled through the federal government. But I found Sam Houston's with no problem on Ancestry.com.

And be careful when you're viewing other people's family trees on Ancestry.com. I found that people have incorrect information posted. As an example; there were two William Harvey Pipkins who fought for Kentucky, one was an officer and one a private. I found that several people who have him on their Walker family tree have the officer, who wasn't married to Nancy Walker but to someone else. Private William Harvey Pipkin who was married to Nancy Walker is the correct individual. And I verified that through his widow's pension.

In some cases to get really detailed Company Muster Cards and pension records you'll have to apply to the National Archives for them. You can get some Muster Cards from Fold3.com but I found them in most cases limited. The National Archives holds the best collection. The same went for Union pension records, which have marriage and death certificates that are great for helping you track down and verify your individual. There is a cost, however, in using the National Archives. For military records they charge $30 per person and for pension records it's $80.

My other favorite resources are books written on your individual's unit. After the Civil War the regiments these men fought with, on both sides, usually got together and held regimental reunions. And a lot had books published about their regimental history during the war. What a great resource! There have also been a lot of books written by authors just like myself who touch on some aspect of the regiment you're looking for. As an example I'm sure anyone looking for information on the 9th Missouri Sharpshooters would find this book helpful in possibly researching their relative. It just takes noodling around and finding what's out there.

And that's how I put this book together. Taking bits and pieces of information that I found from all over the place and tying them together to make a timeline for each brother.

I hope reading this book has motivated you to see what your ancestors were up to during the Civil War!

References

1. Wikipedia.com

2. Muster our roll, Sixth Regiment, Kansas Civil War Volunteers, Volume 7, Company K.

3. The Fort Leavenworth – Fort Gibson Military Road and the Founding of Fort Scott by Louise Barry

4. Missouri State Museum

5. Library of Congress uncredited work

6. www.findagrave.com

7. Ancestry.com

8. Fold3.com

9. The National Archives

10. Texas State Library and Archives Commission

11. James R. O'Neill, 1833 - 1863

12. Fort Smith Museum of History

13. Kansas State Historical Society

14. The Encyclopedia of Arkansas History & Culture

15. Samuel Houston Walker verbal autobiography as written by Madge Daily

16. Letter by Henry S. Carroll Orderly Sergeant, Co. D, 33rd Missouri Volunteer Infantry

17. Letter from Captain John Whitford to his wife. From www.civilwararkansas.blogspot.com By Dale Cox

18. Facebook page "Harvest of Death: The Battle of Jenkins Ferry, Arkansas" by Joe Walker

19. "Shot All to Pieces" by Matt Matthews & Kip Lindberg

20. www.geocities.ws for picture provided by Kay Hively

21. The war of the rebellion: a compilation of the official records of the Union and Confederate armies; series 1 – volumes 22 & 34. By the United States War Department

22. www.ebooks.library.cornell.edu

23. "Centennial History of Missouri" by Walter Barlow Stevens

24. Randy East – Macon County, Tennessee Historian

25. Letter by Napoleon Bonaparte Walker dated the 10th of January 1869 to the U.S. Pension Office

About the author

Ed Semler retired from the United States Coast Guard in December of 2007 with over 25 years of military service in both the United States Army and United States Coast Guard. In the Army he was an enlisted combat bridge crewman (12C) and was honorably discharged as a specialist four (E-4). While in the Coast Guard he was an enlisted machinery technician (MK) obtaining the rank of master chief petty officer (E-9), was commissioned as an officer, and retired as a lieutenant (O-3E).

After his military career Ed dabbled in teaching at a Vocational Technical School and was a self-employed plumber for several years. As a pass time he enjoys reading, writing, and is a proud member of the Schulenburg, Texas chapters of the Veterans of Foreign Wars and American Legion.

Fully retired he resides in Schulenburg, Texas with his wife Jana, a retired Air Force Senior Master Sergeant. Please feel free to contact him at mkcm378@gmail.com or at his website www.edsemler.com

His other publications are;

"Around The World," which details his 25 years of service as an officer and enlisted man in the U.S. Army and U.S. Coast Guard.

"U.S. Coast Guard Cutter Sherman (WHEC-720) Circumnavigation Deployment 2001," which details the Sherman's historic circumnavigation of the globe and deployment to the Persian Gulf in 2001.

"The Three Gunsallus Brothers" which details three brothers fighting for the state of Pennsylvania during the Civil War.

"Thoughts On Being A Chief Petty Officer" which details managing the position of Chief Petty Officer in Coast Guard and Navy.

The author at Sam Houston Walker's grave in Seadrift, Texas

www.ingramcontent.com/pod-product-compliance
Lightning Source LLC
Chambersburg PA
CBHW061332040426
42444CB00011B/2881